THE

Moon
Juice

COOKBOOK

THE

COOKBOOK

COOK COSMICALLY FOR BODY, BEAUTY, AND CONSCIOUSNESS

AMANDA CHANTAL BACON

PHOTOGRAPHS BY JOHN VON PAMER

PAM KRAUSS BOOKS / AVERY

NEW YORK

PAM KRAUSS BOOKS / AVERY
an imprint of Penguin Random House LLC
375 Hudson Street
New York, New York 10014

Most Avery books are available at special quantity discounts
for bulk purchase for sales promotions, premiums, fund-
raising, and educational needs. Special books or book excerpts
also can be created to fit specific needs. For details, write
SpecialMarkets@penguinrandomhouse.com.

ISBN 9780804188203

Printed in China
1 3 5 7 9 10 8 6 4 2

Book design by Marysarah Quinn

FOR MY TEACHERS,
SEEN AND UNSEEN,
ESPECIALLY Rohan

CONTENTS

INTRODUCTION

THE PURSUIT OF HEALTH AND HAPPINESS IN A LIFE OF FOOD

Food can be powerful medicine, and no one has experienced its effects more dramatically than I have. Before I began to cook and eat in a way that allowed me to thrive cosmically, my thyroid was slow, allergies were rampant, and I had the general feeling that I wasn't optimizing this life and the body I was traveling in.

There's nothing I love more than talking to people about the ways in which they can use food as medicine. The moment I lock eyes with someone who is looking to have a greater experience of life and thinks that food may be the most significant environmental factor in achieving that, all I want to do is cheer them along on their journey. I love offering suggestions, tools, and organizational tips that are delicious, exciting, and grounded in common sense. And you will find that and much more in the pages that follow.

As I awakened to the healing potential of food, I realized I wanted to create a space where other people could enjoy the beauty and artistry of food while also gaining access to its medicinal powers. By integrating the advice and tutelage of a group of doctors, healers, and health nuts with my culinary knowledge, my travels, and traditional regional pairings, I knew I could help people target specific health issues. I developed the vision for Moon Juice, a space that would be beautiful, flavor mindful, and truly healing, and a year later we opened our first store, in Venice, California.

From the start, I wanted Moon Juice to be a place for everyone—not just yogis and vegans, but also those who had eaten with abandon the night before and might come in nursing hangovers, or people on a first date wanting to indulge in something mood altering that didn't include caffeine or alcohol. A place where people could learn how to make simple yet life-changing additions to their diet, rather than be preached to about limiting themselves. And most important, I wanted it to be a source for the most medicinally potent foods that delivered the earth's beautiful flavors and textures.

Today, Moon Juice supplies an active global Moon Family with foods, potions, and lifestyle tools. Moon Juice excites and inspires people looking to get on the path and satiates those like myself who are already down the rabbit hole. Our products are organic, plant based, super nutrient dense, high functioning, and always activated (sprouted). The delicious recipes often include elements from Ayurvedia and traditional Chinese medicine wrapped up into flavor profiles and techniques from

my fine-dining days. Our original focus on juices and plant-based milks has broadened to encompass an extensive range of cosmic provisions, and Moon Dusts.

When I compose a recipe, I find inspiration in both the far-flung and the unadulterated flavors found at local farmers' markets. I take my cues from traditional pairings, chefs I have worked with, holistic and intuitive remedies, and my own desire to create beauty on the plate and on the palate. Every Moon Juice, milk, or cookie should taste extraordinary as it works synergistically to heal and nourish your physical form, brain function, and spirit at the deepest level.

This isn't a book about everything you should abstain from and

remove from your life. This is just a cookbook filled with really delicious recipes that will give you new range in the kitchen. The only difference here is that when you become seduced by the flavors and the process of making these foods and begin to eat them often, you will begin to experience pretty radical life shifts and contribute to the health of our earth.

Discovering the ways in which foods can be healing, and coming to recognize what is empowering to your system will help you to tune your palate. It may take some trial and error to find your own best path, but I'll be there to help you every step of the way, acting as the kind of guide I wish I'd had on my own journey to regaining my health and vitality.

I'd love to sit with you and show you how easy it can be. I want to feed you raw chocolate bites, and get a coconut yoghurt culturing on your countertop as we unpack the dehydrator that just arrived in the mail.

I want to be the one who gets to hug you as you tell me you actually really like the taste of unsweetened green juice, and that maybe world peace really does start in the kitchen. Until we have the opportunity to cross paths, this book is for you, and your friends, and their friends, and the hundreds of thousands of new friends we haven't met yet. It contains everything I'd tell you if we were together and you told me you wanted to change your life. There is a vast, beautiful world of live medicinal foods for you to explore. Let your body learn with joy. As you feed yourself plants, good fats, minerals, and enzymes, you will feel inspired and satiated on very fundamental levels, and begin to settle into an emotional well-being that you won't want to disrupt.

People always ask if I knew Moon Juice would be so successful, and to be honest, I did. There is a cosmic calling and powerful movement here to push us forward as a race. A big part of the movement is caring for our bodies, as well as for the health of our planet. Anytime we make a move toward supporting or joining that mission, we tune in to the flow of otherworldly success and abundance. That's what Moon Juice really is—not just a product or a place but rather a healing force, an etheric potion, and a cosmic beacon for the evolutionary movement of seeking beauty, happiness, and longevity. I've written this book so that you can have your own profound experience with live and organic plant foods as delicious medicine that nourishes and heals the body from the inside out. This is more than a collection of recipes; it's a love story. Let the romance of ritual, flavor, and cosmic energy lure you into a plant-rich, lively diet that will ignite your intuition, radiance, and inspiration. I can't wait for you to experience the life that blossoms on the outside to mirror the vibrant good health you are experiencing on the inside.

Let me be a bridge between the world of medicine and the pleasures and rituals of fine dining and familial ceremonies. How do medicine and prevention converge with pleasure and emotion? How do we build the new traditions and rituals to support that convergence? This book will show you how. We can make this exciting, easy, and graceful. It should be joyful. You will be able to take this information, integrate it as truth, and work it into your lifestyle. You will become the alchemist.

CHAPTER I

BECOMING THE ALCHEMIST

EATING TO BE HAPPY, HEALTHY, AND BEAUTIFUL

Diet is a powerful tool that can help you awaken, receive, and increase life-force energy. When we think of healthy eating, we typically assume there will be weight loss, enhanced glow, and increased strength, but that pales in comparison to the paradigm shift that begins with plant nutrition.

Moon Juice came into being as a way for me to share the life-changing effects of my journey to wellness, a journey that led me not only around the world and back, but to a food-centered lifestyle that has enabled me to thrive in a way I never thought possible. It took me some time to find my voice and the strength to walk a path that wasn't always clear or rewarding in the beginning, but I had faith that a better version of health and happiness was available to me. And gaining an understanding of how certain foods led directly to my happiness while others worked against it launched me on what I know will be a lifelong quest for practices that will help my body thrive and that also bring me pleasure.

This quest started at an early age when I experienced a health crisis that could not be resolved despite many trips to doctors and many rounds of pink bubble gum–flavored antibiotics. I had a cough that kept me up at night and difficulty breathing. My parents were at a loss.

One day my family was shopping for groceries in a health food store when my hacking cough drew attention from a number of strangers, including a kind-looking man who asked me to stick out my tongue and took my pulse. He turned out to be an Ayurvedic physician from India, and within minutes he had made a diagnosis and delineated for my mother all the foods I should avoid—the primary ones being wheat, cow's milk, and sugar.

For me, at five, this news was devastating: sugary cereal, bagels, and pizza were the fundamental building blocks of any New York kid's diet. What would I do at sleepovers and birthday parties? After a week of the new regimen, though, my symptoms disappeared completely. I quickly learned that what I put in my body directly affected my quality of life.

As I grew, my immune system also became stronger, so I was able to have some moments of flexibility, but even then I always felt it the next day, and I was susceptible to bronchitis, chronic sinusitis, and terrible allergies. As I moved into my teens, I began to receive warnings from Western medical practitioners, which became diagnoses of exhaustion, hormonal imbalance, and emotional distress ranging from ADD, Hashimoto's thyroiditis (a form of hypothyroidism), auto-immune disorders, depression, pre-diabetes, and a whole range of other maladies. All these diagnoses came with the message that it was a lifelong sentence that could only be addressed with synthetic drugs, and that failing to take those drugs would ultimately be life threatening.

Despite my radical food restrictions as a child, I was developing a deeper appreciation for food in all its many aspects. From my father, who was attending French culinary school at the time, I learned about exotic ingredients. When my family joined a CSA on Long Island, where I spent summers, I discovered farming, and spent my days biking through corn and potato fields and picking tomatoes. I lingered in the kitchen on summer afternoons, transfixed by the simple precision of my father's cooking and the pristinely fresh, vibrantly delicious flavor of the local produce. I remember the joy of floating strawberries in the sink to remove the dirt before we used them to make ice cream. Picking the food that I would be eating was my idea of heaven.

From the exceptional restaurants of New York City, I discovered food's power to enchant. Even more than the dishes themselves, I loved the rituals around food, candlelight, the clinking of forks, the attire, and the connections sustained over a meal.

In my late teens and early twenties, traveling through Europe, the South Pacific, and South America, I learned the exquisite flavors of true peasant food. I saw that rustic Italian food, with its few ingredients, bountiful vegetables, legumes, and just-picked herbs, could be more profound than any flavors I had tasted before. And I learned how transformative culinary technique could be from watching the son of a fisherman in a tiny seaside restaurant in Uruguay cook vegetables on the grill, as he explained the importance of sourcing the right wood and paying attention to the way the fire was built, the embers, the time between when the produce was picked and when it was cooked, and the exact way in which they were cut.

When I eventually returned to the United States, it was to enroll in culinary school. I chose a school that was the first to engage food politics in the curriculum. The instructors focused on food quality, and spoke about the importance of farm-to-table cooking before it was a nationwide movement. When I wasn't in the classroom, I spent my time working at an artisanal bakery, and helping out on a farm and in a dairy. I was deeply challenged, but I loved it. After graduation I moved to California, deeply inspired by the work of Alice Waters, who invited me to her table, and Suzanne Goin, who gave me a spot on her kitchen staff.

As stimulated as I was by these culinary heroes, I was also testing my luck with my health. Working in kitchens, I had become accustomed to a lifestyle that included not just wheat, sugar, and dairy, but tons of wine, coffee, and a whole lot of sleep deprivation coupled with a great amount of stress. My immunity and energy were low, I had awful seasonal allergies, and I was experiencing a host of other symptoms, from anxiety to temper flare-ups to—of course—my familiar bronchial issues.

I decided things had to change when I noticed the extent of my sugar addiction and had done enough research to see that it was directly affecting my adrenals and thyroid gland. After a day of not having any refined sugar, I found myself rummaging through the fridge at midnight to spoon jelly straight from the jar. I realized I needed help.

I had read about how effective juice cleanses could be in resetting the body, and in Italy I started drinking raw, pressed fruit juices. Sitting down to a beautiful glass of blood orange or white peach juice was a highlight of my day. I took this mind-set with me to New Zealand, where I started drinking green juices made with touches of apple and lemon. I didn't start juicing at home, though, until I moved to California and a friend loaned me his vintage Champion Juicer. I immediately made green juices with arugula that powered my days in the kitchen, and began to help me reconnect to my body and mind in places where I had disconnected.

It was through Dr. Norman Walker's 1970s book, *Fresh Vegetable and Fruit Juices*, that I started to recognize the synergy of pressing specific herbs, vegetables, and fruits together to address distinct health challenges. The potential for alchemizing juices in this way, and adapting them to my own palate and flavor preferences, was exciting.

What was supposed to be a few days of drinking juices turned into a week, and then into a twenty-one-day cleanse. The clarity and energy I felt from the juices, teas, lemon water, vegetable broth, smoothies made of greens and seaweed, and raw green vegetables I ate during that time ignited something in me, and brought me back to the way I had felt when I was a child—before I got sick. After just a few days on the cleanse, I found I had more energy than ever before. I could taste flavors in ways I never had, and for the first time in years, my sleep was incredible. One of the most challenging parts of being a cook was feeling beaten up at the end of the day, drinking a bottle of wine, going to bed, and getting up close to noon feeling like I hadn't slept at all. But on the nonstop juice party, I was functioning on a completely different level, and I wasn't having the obsessive thoughts about sugar, wheat, and dairy I had been having.

I realized that I never again wanted my life to get so far off track that I would feel disconnected from true health and happiness. In some ways, I had forgotten what it really felt like to be happy and healthy; low energy, allergies, skin conditions, and fluctuating moods felt normal to me.

When I found myself again through food and medicinal herbs, I resolved to bridge the gap between the healing world and the foodie world for others, just as I had for myself. I felt revolution coming, and I wanted to align myself with the energy force-feeding this shift in consciousness. I found my focus and what turned out to be my life's work: to serve people and support them in an entirely new way through food.

So I sought out doctors, acupuncturists, and naturopaths, and began studying under healthcare practitioners who had cured people of serious ailments with food, juice, and herbs. I read every book I could on the subject, and absorbed as much as possible from individuals who were

generous enough to answer my constant stream of questions. I learned to supplement my diet with adaptogens, some of the first medicinal herbs I learned about—foods with nutritional properties that stabilize physiological and hormonal processes in the body. I made my own almond milk and blended it with cacao (raw chocolate, which is energizing and mineralizing) and maca. I sweetened these milks with stevia, an herb that is two hundred times as sweet as sugar but doesn't affect blood sugar levels. Seaweed helped supply my body with iodine, one of the minerals that boosts thyroid hormone production. Within a few months of this new regimen, I noticed a radical shift—my period, which had been irregular and largely absent for years, finally returned. And my next round of bloodwork revealed that my thyroid hormone levels were back to normal.

Eating a live, plant-based, organic diet completely changed my life and has proven to be the most fun, delicious, and beautiful medicine I've ever taken. And the changes weren't all physical. I noticed that the inclusion of green juices and live plant foods in my diet incited a personality shift. Thought patterns and roles I had assumed were part of my "personality" dissolved. These apparently deep-seated traits of mine were disappearing just as my cough had vanished in the absence of sugar, wheat, and dairy.

With organic, live plant foods flooding my system, I started to have a general expansion in all aspects of my life, inwardly and outwardly. The foods I was choosing were changing the nature of the thoughts that were creating my reality. I was able to access a really happy and high energy. Over time, it became clear that much of my "personality" and attachment to certain struggles that held me back from bliss had a lot to do with what I was experiencing on a cellular level. With an alkaline system full of minerals, enzymes, and good fats, I began to react to life triggers differently. The live plant foods and medicinal herbs I fed myself gave me a new sensitivity and access to a subtle yet powerful energy force. This is what ultimately led to the birth of Moon Juice, as I became aware that there could be nothing better for me to do with my days than to share this new wealth with others.

While I strongly believe in food as art and entertainment, I've found a world of pleasure in foods that don't hurt the body and can actually heal. I believe there is sustenance in creativity and that simplicity can be exquisite. All these factors come into play when you explore the principles of Moon Juice, and this book is your road map.

Rest assured, however, that Moon Juice is not about labels or dietary restrictions. I don't claim to be vegan, though I do eat that way most of the time. The more live plant foods I eat, the more I crave food charged with enzymes, minerals, proteins, vitamins, and good fats—and the more readily I can access vital energy, a positive, meditative nature, and stellar physical form. You don't need to be all raw, nor should you feel bad about eating cooked food; raw food is just a really potent tool you can add to your life and experiment with depending on your needs. Balancing long nights of decadence with a day or a week of more raw foods can be complementary in the same way wakefulness and sleep are when they are in balance. I trust that I will make the right decisions for myself, and after reading this book, you will, too. There may be times when a seasonal change inspires you to eat mostly raw foods—for example, warm weather begets raw, hydrating foods. If you are feeling taxed, stressed, or physically exhausted from travel, work, or overindulgence, your body may crave foods loaded with enzymes that are less work to digest and will help to brighten you up. Other times you'll fold those foods into cooked meals simply because they are so delicious. There's no reason you can't include our macadamia nut cheese alongside your other favorite cheeses on a cheese board. My approach, one I urge you to embrace, is to remain open to each day and the opportunities that arise, leaving room to enjoy special occasions without guilt. This is a lifestyle, not a road map to some perfect fixed state, and if it is not enjoyable and flexible, you won't be successful. You will see the greatest benefits and pleasures from eating from the Moon Kitchen when it becomes a beloved practice.

HEALTHY IS NOT A FIXED STATE BUT AN ENRICHING, LIFELONG JOURNEY

Acknowledging to myself that there is no such thing as a fixed state of perfect health has been humbling. For a while I thought that if I could just abstain from everything "bad," maintain a perfect meditation practice,

have a perfectly cultured gut in a perpetually alkaline state, and basically learn everything I would have had I gone to medical school, I would achieve perfect health and the dial would just stay there. (I'm sure if I dug a little deeper into that fantasy, I would see that perfect state of health also encompassed having a perfectly tidy house, with a perfect family.) Now I know that health is not an ultimate destination; it's a lifelong pursuit. Even when we work really hard to be our healthiest selves, we face struggles and experiences that we can't quite figure out—no matter how much green juice we drink. According to my Western medical diagnoses over the years, I have an autoimmune condition, chronic allergies, attention deficit disorder, depression, anxiety—and I'm sure that list would have kept going had I not taken my body on this joyful journey and daily culinary practice. This way of cooking and feasting works, I promise you. With the help of a great team that assists me in making choices about how best to support a thyroid that fluctuates between normal and low function, I continue to refine my diet and health practices. There have certainly been times when I was feeling on top of the world and put my system to the test, thinking maybe I had magically "cured" myself, only to slide into an inflammatory state by overindulging in sweets and inviting stress into my system. On those occasions, though, I've quickly been reminded that my health is a living ecosystem that requires my participation to function well.

I should say at this point that anybody can benefit from this kind of diet, not just those who share my health issues. For some, it may be an investment in longevity that gives them a polished glow now; for others, it can lead to weight loss and access to a new line of joy and strength. For those like myself, it may really come down to a change of destiny, a choice to fight against the odds and believe you can have peace of mind and vitality in the face of "disease," whether strictly through diet, or as an integral part of medical treatment. And I am not discounting the possibility that you are just into insanely awesome raw chocolate and will be taken by surprise when you notice that you have surges of energy, an ignited libido, and toned skin once you start eating more of these foods.

EATING FOR THE FUTURE WHILE COMMANDING YOUR NOW

It used to be that most people would create a lifestyle around health due to some type of health crisis. I'm now seeing a mass shift in consciousness as people no longer feel the need to reach a crisis point before they make a choice to live more consciously. They're coming to me in health, wanting to figure out how to amplify and preserve their vitality and radiance. There is a movement of reclaiming our birthright of health and happiness and beauty on this planet. Within this larger framework for getting into our highest states of grace, there are specific ingredients that can be used to target tissue regrowth, promote gut health that leads to glowing skin, herbs that encourage hair growth, liver cleansers that yield sparkling white eyes, mineral-dense foods that feed the skin, and nerve tonics that can help to calm the system and relax the face.

One of the founding principles of Moon Juice is that prevention and maintenance are the most direct path to wellness. We may work with the expertise of healers and doctors when needed, but we can't blindly turn ourselves over to their care and expect to be fixed. Our own personal library of information, experiences, and experimentation is what enables us to cook and care for our needs and our loved ones more intuitively. We need to step into our power and feel responsible for our own health.

I find that the most powerful and practical step in health is education; without truly knowing why we are striving to eat the way we eat, the practice is not as meaningful or as profound. When you truly under-stand what's happening on the plate, in the body, and in the mind, there is a new motivation. The understanding of how all the parts work to make you look better, feel better, live longer, become fascinating. And when you start to see these things occur and can trace these changes back to the foods you are eating, that's when the ball really starts rolling.

Education is key because when you build a strong foundation, you won't need to eat this way at every meal if you don't feel like it. But it will be empowering for you to know the ins and outs of what makes you function well and what are some of the foods that you know don't suit your body and can cause little things to go off in your system. You will be well equipped should something go awry like a skin condition, low immunity, or disrupted sleeping patterns or moods—you won't be left disturbed and wondering. You will have control and will be able to steer yourself back in the right direction before you find yourself at the doc-tor—or in a heap of tears on the floor.

BEAUTY AND BALANCE

I'm often asked to share my beauty regimen. My answer is that beauty is not a regimen but a state of grace and longevity that follows biological age, not chronological age. We are beautiful when we are healthy, happy, loving, high functioning, and vital. That's a different size and shape for each of us, uniquely and radiantly your own. It consists of a diet that includes a lot of raw plants and good fats, cultured foods, Moon Dusts, raw chocolate, meditation, and a commitment to keeping an open, lov-ing heart. My advice is to put your whole life behind it and love it!

THE TEN TENETS
OF THE MOON KITCHEN

In health, many things feel overly complicated, but there are just ten foundations on which all the teachings of the Moon Kitchen are based. They are not listed in any particular order, as they work together holisti-cally and synergistically.

1

GET RAW

to load up on enzymes, minerals, and phytonutrients for energy, digestion, and glow.

2

GET ALKALIZED

to balance your pH, making your body an inhospitable environment for disease.

3

MINERALIZE

to give your brain and body the nutrients they need to thrive.

4

GET GOOD FAT

to nourish the brain and nervous system, and create vital energy.

5

SLOW YOUR GLYCEMIC ROLL

by limiting sugar in all forms.

6

REWILD THYSELF

by nurturing your gut flora with cultured and fermented foods.

7

EMBRACE ENZYMES

to supply your body with the amino acids and the enzyme cofactors needed to boost your own natural enzyme production.

8

AMINO-FY

Stock up on staples like activated nuts and seeds—spirulina, sea veggies, dark leafy greens, bee pollen, and nutritional yeast.

9

ADOPT ADAPTOGENS

which help the body to be in harmony by adapting to stress and change.

10

VOTE ORGANIC

to ensure the food you eat is free of pesticides and other chemicals and contaminants.

EAT MORE RAW

A raw food is anything that has not been heated above 115 degrees Fahrenheit, preserving the living enzymes. There are so many benefits to eating raw foods: abundant energy, sharpened brain power, glowing skin, lifted spirits, and restored digestion and assimilation. It's not necessary to become a raw foodist or forego cooked foods altogether to harness the power of raw foods; getting the benefits of raw foods is as simple as eating a whole fruit or vegetable. Just eat as many raw foods as you can each day, choosing what is in season and what you're craving.

GET ALKALIZED

Disease creeps into acidic states, and existing in an alkaline state is key to maintaining a calm and joyful life. Alkalinity creates an overall glow, with radiant skin and sparkling eyes, and also supports our desires to rewild; you can't richly culture your gut if it's in an acidic state. You'll find some of my favorite alkaline foods in this book, but the basics of an alkaline diet have already been color coded for you by nature: The greener, the better.

MINERALIZE

Eating an abundance of mineral-rich foods like activated nuts and seeds, pink salt, cacao, leafy greens, bananas, sweet potatoes, figs, seaweed, almonds, chia, sesame seeds, pumpkin seeds, and mulberries is truly the best way to enhance and sustain beauty and joy. Becoming mineralized will soothe inflammation, tame degeneration, and fully activate enzymes in the cells, providing critical components of collagen and connective tissue, which provide elasticity and flexibility and nourishment to tissues like skin, hair, and nails for that radiant glow. Calcium, magnesium, zinc, and copper are needed to make the proteins essential for our existence and for keeping our bones healthy. Bioavailable minerals like magnesium and calcium are key to calming the nerves, lowering blood pressure, aiding healthy sleep cycles, and taming anxiety. Minerals like iron impact mood, energy, and

life experience in that they shuttle oxygen to the brain and provide energy to the body. Dietary staples like calcium and iron have actually been shown to be more abundant in raw plants than in their animal-based counterparts, and your body can assimilate them just as effectively—without the bad fats, acidity, and environmental impact associated with animal products.

GOOD FATS

We need good fat for brain function, hormone production, metabolism, weight loss, energy, immune function, and inflammatory response. Sixty percent of the brain is made up of fat, and the fat you eat literally feeds your brain, aiding neurological functions and the mental clarity that enables you to live a healthy, happy, inspired life.

Heat changes the fatty acid chain and oxidizes these molecules, creating degenerated fats that are difficult to digest, harder for the system to process, and often read as more acidic in the body.

Raw plant fats like avocado, coconut, nuts, seeds, green juice (yes, green juice contains fat, in the form of omega-3s), and olive oil are energizing, brain powering, nervous system supporting, beautifying, cleansing, and immunity building. These fats are also great ways to deliver fat-soluble vitamins and nutrients while cleansing us of fat-soluble toxins.

Fats also help with hormonal balance by acting as hormone receptors. Contrary to how we have been trained as a culture to think of fat as fattening, properly eating fat can help you reduce fat levels in the body.

My diet is 40 to 60 percent fat, depending on my energy requirements for the day. This may sound shocking coming from someone who's known for guzzling green juice, but I am a strong believer in empowering fat. We all went through some "fat-free" consciousness in the nineties. After it became clear that carbing out on packaged foods and purging with aspartame wasn't looking good, there was the next freakish fad, which implored you to eat bacon and only bacon. I like to call this recalibration we are all having "post-fat-free." It's important to have some context into which to put this rediscovered love of and healing with fat. I believe in a low-glycemic, plant-based diet featuring a lot of raw foods. I really emphasize the low-glycemic part; I eliminated grains from my normal routine, and am very careful to read the sugar content in any prepared whole foods I eat. I have done this with reverence for food as an art form and still deeply enjoy special-occasion desserts and grain, not for physical nourishment, but as part of a conscious act of pleasure.

I work nonstop and have a small child; I'm on a mission and it's go, go, go. My body and brain couldn't keep up with my life if I followed a low-fat regimen. I have personally felt the effects of getting enough good, healthy fats into my diet, and it has radically enhanced my energy, stabilized my hormones, and nourished my nervous system. A word of caution: As you are increasing your healthy fats you'll want to become mindful of how many grams of sugar you are consuming over the course of a day.

LOW GLYCEMIC

Making sure that my everyday is low sugar and my high-sugar moments are conscious choices made in a balanced bigger picture is so very important for letting my endocrine system, vital organs, and gut health thrive in an unstressed fashion. I prepare the bulk of my foods with this intention and always read sugar counts on prepared whole foods. Eating in a low-glycemic fashion also supports rewilding your digestive system with desired bacteria and not candida, which feasts on sugar. It's also essential as a basis for a diet rich in good fats, as a high-sugar/high-fat diet does not work. Supplementing my low-glycemic diet with fermented foods caused the biggest leap I've experienced in my health and happiness. Fermented foods will actually support your backing off sugar if you have a sweet tooth. When a craving hits, try having a glass of kefir or a bit of fermented veggies instead of a sugary treat. You will immediately notice brain clarity, elevated energy, tamed inflammation, glowing skin, and access to a steady, calm happiness. Adopting organic stevia into my kitchen was another real game changer; I make most of my "sweets" with stevia and use it every day in my Moon Milks.

PROBIOTICS

Your gut accounts for two-thirds of your immune system and is the true foundation of health, happiness, and beauty. Fermented foods are a superlative source of enzymes and probiotics that nurture intestinal microflora, heal the gut, and recolonize the intestines with organisms that defend against disease, viruses, and yeast. These immunity-building foods improve digestion and nutrient absorption, create glowing skin, and improve your mood and brain function. Rewilding is most delicious and cost effective with fermented foods like cultured veggies, nut cheeses, coconut kefir, and yoghurt rather than probiotic supplements that may not be very potent depending on how long they've been on a shelf. I eat them in various delicious forms at least once a day to cultivate healthy, healing bacteria.

ENZYMATIC

Enzymes are catalysts for your body's basic biochemical functions, like building raw materials, distributing nutrients, and removing unwanted chemicals. They are also required in biological functions that are necessary for really critical actions like energy production, wound healing and infection fighting, inflammation taming, nutrient assimilation, detoxing, hormone balance, and slowing the aging process. These essential amino acids are either produced by your body or obtained from food. The more raw foods you eat, the less burden there is on your body to produce all the enzymes it needs to thrive. The most powerfully enzyme-rich foods are activated and sprouted nuts and seeds, but pineapple, papaya, mango, avocado, raw honey and bee pollen, olive oil, and coconut oil are all good sources of enzymes. I love to add ghee to this list; it's the superconductor in enzyme production. The more, the merrier, enzymatically speaking, because enzymes not used in the digestive process get straight to work on other vital functions.

Digestive enzymes break down your food so that it may be better assimilated into every cell in your body. These enzymes are extracellular, which means they are found outside your cell walls. Metabolic enzymes are intracellular, found inside your cells, and carry out functions related to cellular reproduction and vitality.

Besides breaking down food, digestive enzymes are busy with gut healing, beauty making, mood stabilization, energizing, metabolism boosting, pathogen control, brain function, and immune support.

The other types of enzymatic activity require metabolic enzymes. These intracellular enzymes are necessary for running your circulatory (blood), lymphatic, cardiac, neurologic, endocrine (thyroid and adrenal), renal (kidney), hepatic (liver), and reproductive systems, as well as maintaining tissues like skin, bones, joints, brain, and muscles. They are specifically useful in blood cleansing, catalyzing energy production, transcribing DNA into RNA, and combatting inflammation, which is at the root of all chronic disease.

In short, we eat these delicious foods for pleasure, beauty, and vitality. A great deal of that happy energetic glow is due to the supreme enzyme counts in these live and purposefully potent recipes.

AMINO-FIED

Amino acids are made of carbon, hydrogen, and oxygen; they bond together to make long chains. Those long chains of hundreds to thousands of amino acids are called proteins, the workhorse nutrients of life, critical to happy, healthy, energetic bodies. Even though more than fifty amino acids have been discovered, only twenty are used to make protein. Of those twenty, our cells can make eleven of the amino acids it needs from other molecules in your body; nine are categorized as essential because the body can't synthesize them, so we have to get them from the food. Thousands of combinations of those twenty are

used to make more than one hundred thousand types of proteins in our body, which make up 75 percent of our dry weight. Protein builds lean muscles, lets us feel satiated, gives metabolism a boost by taking more energy to break down and digest than carbohydrates, and aids our cells in tissue growth and repair. Protein is literally the building block of life. Specific plants are the best suited for the job, and will build flexible muscle and neurotransmitters for proper brain chemistry.

A point of concern for some wanting to consume more plant foods is they don't provide enough protein, and plant-based protein is incomplete. Different types of plant proteins have different amino acid profiles, and our bodies actually create the exact proteins required, when required, and they do this from amino acids, not protein. Our body naturally pools amino acids together from the array of foods we eat and naturally creates proteins for us. Protein is broken down by the body; it's the middleman that provides the amino acids we need.

It can be very efficient to eat raw plants to get those amino acids. We can eat an intelligent selection of fruits, veggies, nuts, and seeds throughout our life without worrying about combining things properly to create complete proteins, and the body will collect and combine the amino acids to create the proteins. It's not necessary to "combine proteins" (like the rice and bean theory) in the same meal, provided you eat a combination of different plant protein sources throughout the day, but it is necessary to make sure you are getting ample amounts of certain amino acids so your body is not limited in being able to build proteins. This is where the rice and beans theory comes in, as they provide amino acids lysine and methionine, which are the common missing elements of a plant-based diet.

The best way to take care of your amino and protein intake with confidence is to meet your caloric requirements with a varied rainbow diet of organic fruits and vegetables (especially dark greens), nuts, seeds, and activated foods. I mentally tick off my boxes for lysine with spirulina, nuts—pistachios and pumpkin seeds in particular—quinoa, amaranth, buckwheat, oatmeal, kale, romaine lettuce, spinach, broccoli, avocados, tomatoes, and oranges. You should aim to eat 50 to 100 grams of protein a day (depending on your activity level and body size), which is easily attainable with plants foods.

ADAPTOGENIC

Adaptogens help the body to be in harmony with its environment by adapting to stress and change. Mineral-dense adaptogens allow your body to absorb nutrients, maintaining the body's optimum energy and metabolism, increasing immunity and libido, easing inflammation, and balancing depression and anxiety. My pantry is stocked with adaptogenic herbs so I can easily blend them into hot or cold nut milk throughout the day as a major pick-me-up or even a meal. Depending on what my body is specifically needing, I will sprinkle them into batches of raw chocolate or puddings to bring the medicine cabinet into the kitchen in a delighful way.

ORGANIC

The recipes in this book are all born from a celebration of whole, organic ingredients, finding intuition and flow in the kitchen, and a journey in the revolution to support ourselves. In this era of big business and industrial agricultural practices, it's important to advocate for organics. Everything we make and sell at Moon Juice is completely organic or wildcrafted. This is something I chose not only for the health of my customers, but for the health of our planet. Since making this commitment, I no longer have allergies; I don't get sick nearly as often, and when I do, my recovery times are short. My moods are better, my skin glows, and my digestion is dreamy. Granted, this commitment to eating organic is a facet to a lifestyle, but it is an integral component of my overall health practices.

USE YOUR NATURAL INTUITION TO HEAL

We are all born to be alchemists. Tune in and let the reconnection to the wilderness of your being begin. As you bring more of these functional foods into your life and get to know them, you will reconnect to your body's perfect intuition and the energies of the plants you work with.

Don't be surprised if you find yourself beginning to crave the ones you need most each day. The chart that follows lists the categories I have found I am asked about most often, plus suggestions on which foods are most effective in nourishing them specifically. The recipes in this book were created for targeted results within these categories, and each is marked accordingly so you can let your eyes guide you and feed your whims, or filter through the pages seeking out specific remedies for the condition you wish to address.

At the beginning, though, you just want to start training your brain and your palate to be the alchemist. When you gain mastery over the simple principles of cooking and eating in the Moon Kitchen—along the way becoming happier, more focused, and energized—you can build on this base of very powerful eating habits to become even more strategic. The body and mind are completely holistic entities; there is no beauty without proper brain chemistry, there is no brainpower without a healthy body, and there are countless microfunctions in all the systems that speak to one another. We are an incredibly complex symphony of a machine in a highly controlled biosphere.

You may start to clog the free-flowing energy. When energy becomes blocked in certain areas, it sets off a domino effect. It may be subtle at first, but it can escalate into something you can see and feel. I really look at health and beauty as something that already lives inside of me; there are times in our lives when we just need to realign with that perfection. And this perfectly potent plant-based alchemy is a tool to help your body and mind remember its own perfection. This system is a way in which you can begin to train your mind and your palate to home in on these ingredients. I really think of each ingredient as affecting the body and mind and everything in between all at once, always, but this is an overwhelming starting point. Through this chart we have highlighted its primary function as benefiting either body, brain, or beauty. Once you choose an ingredient based on the primary function you are interested in, you will discover its secondary and possibly tertiary benefits. As you begin to discover, cook, and taste these elements and experience the particular effects they have on you, you will inherently begin to catalog all this data, and the holistic nature of both your system and the plant systems will become more clear.

There is a lot of knowledge out there on these potent ingredients, and food alchemy can be overwhelming if approached in a purely intellectual way. This book is really designed to be an experiential guide and inspiration for incorporating them into your everyday diet; I simply have not found reading about them and taking them in pill form empowering in the same way. I have provided enough information here for you to get cooking and understanding how you can use them to revive and restore your body, brain, and beauty. When you begin cooking with these benefits in mind, dishes inspired by medicinal plants will be savored as your new true comfort food. You will be having the direct experience of being the alchemist, which, in turn, will give you an intimate understanding of ingredients and an unshakeable confidence when it comes to incorporating them into your daily life. It's truly through experience that you will find your own alchemist.

HIGH-FUNCTIONING FOODS

The Moon Pantry is powered by an array of high-functioning, bioavailable, potent, medicinal, whole foods with unique flavor profiles and mouthfeels. These foods are packed with exceptionally high levels of vitamins, minerals, antioxidants, and enzymes, turning them into tools we can use to tone, nourish, and empower our bodies. These foods heal your cells, protect against oxidation, slow the aging process, and support your immune system by stimulating and supplementing your body's disease- and infection-fighting properties. After years of working with this group of high-functioning foods, I not only found myself relying on them as part of a health, beauty, and wellness routine, but actually craving the earthy flavors and the silky textures they bring to the kitchen. Add them to your morning smoothie or enrich your meals and snacks throughout the day.

POWER FOODS

ASHWAGANDHA
ADAPTOGEN. THYROID SUPPORT. STRESS RELIEVER.
Ashwagandha is a potent root that calms. This mineral-dense adaptogen aids thyroid function, alleviates depression, improves sleep, and contributes to virility.

BEE POLLEN
ENERGY FOOD. HORMONE BALANCER. APHRODISIAC.
Bee pollen is a mystical dance between flowers and bees that yields a predigested, easily assimilated, alkaline food dense with antioxidants, minerals, vitamins, twenty-two amino acids, and bioavailable proteins. High levels of vitamin B combat acne and wrinkles, while pollen alleviates allergy symptoms. A potent aphrodisiac, blood nourisher, and muscle food, bee pollen supports fertility and stamina, muscle growth and definition, and recovery from exercise.

BLUE-GREEN ALGAE AND BLUE ALGAE
PLANT PROTEIN. DETOXIFIER. BRAIN ACTIVATOR.
One of the most nutrient-dense foods on this blue-green earth. This is a protein-rich, biologically active chlorophyll, with a complete spectrum of amino acids. It's an extremely energizing, alkalizing, deeply mineralizing, inflammation-soothing immunity food.

CACAO
JOY PROMOTER. APHRODISIAC. METABOLISM BOOSTER.
Cacao's divine mineralizing medicine is powerful, intoxicating, and high functioning. Feel the rush of blissful endorphins and mood-boosting hormones; antioxidants increase brain flow, boost metabolism, nourish your nervous system, battle fatigue, and spark libido. Raw cacao can be enjoyed as nibs (I like to use them as a crunchy chocolate chip garnish) or in powdered form.

CHAGA
ADAPTOGEN. IMMUNITY FOOD. INFLAMMATION TAMER.
Wild chaga mushroom protects against DNA damage and oxidation; slows the aging process; supports glowing skin, eyes, and hair; and encourages well-being. The cell-strengthening power of this potent immunizing, nourishing, anti-inflammatory mushroom also fuels recovery and longevity.

CORDYCEPS
ADAPTOGEN. IMMUNITY FOOD. HORMONE BALANCER.
Cordyceps mushroom exponentially increases

cellular oxygen absorption, boosting the immune system and making this a powerful tonic for strength, stamina, energy, and lung and brain function.

HO SHOU WU

ADAPTOGEN. HORMONE BALANCER. BEAUTY FOOD.
Ho shou wu is an herb tonic that has been used for centuries to enhance youthfulness, reproductive function, and sex drive. Its potent effects stimulate and balance hormones, improve adrenal gland function, and nourish skin, hair, and internal organs for total glow.

LUCUMA

BEAUTY FOOD. INFLAMMATION TAMER. MINERALIZES DEEPLY.
Lucuma delivers the soothing benefits of this fruit in the most bioavailable form possible. It's an active wound healer and tissue regenerator, reversing the effects of aging and inflammation. Our lucuma is loaded with vitamins and minerals, fiber, and iron. It's sweet and luscious flavor complements other Moon Pantry foods and herbs.

MACA

ADAPTOGEN. HORMONE BALANCER. METABOLISM BOOSTER.
Maca is a Peruvian root, and helps the body adapt to stress by countering the negative effects of tension and anxiety while tonifying and boosting the endocrine system. Maca delivers abundant energy, mental stamina, hormonal balance, enhanced libido, and an elevated mood. Maca's nutty and complex caramel flavor complements other Moon Pantry foods and herbs.

MATCHA

BRAIN ACTIVATOR. METABOLISM BOOSTER. JOY PROMOTER.
This grassy powder made from Japanese whole leaf tea is an incredible flavor to play with and a potent source of caffeine. I love to pair it with sesame, coconut, and cardamom. It packs a seriously nourishing energy and brain chemistry boost that lifts the mood. It's very rich in

chlorophyll, alkalizing, cleansing, and supportive to the holistic vision. Matcha actually increases your metabolic rate, helping you to burn fat. It's a sustainable plant solution that won't wear on your adrenals, an extremely important consideration when you are looking to lose weight.

MUCUNA PRURIENS

BRAIN ACTIVATOR. JOY PROMOTER. STRESS RELIEVER.
Mucuna is a bioavailable source of L-dopa, an amino acid that becomes the neurotransmitter dopamine in the brain. This bean deftly elevates mood, creativity, libido, and sleep patterns, while soothing the nervous system. Mucuna's caramel flavor is a delicious complement to other Moon Pantry foods and herbs.

PEARL

ADAPTOGEN. MINERALIZES DEEPLY. BEAUTY FOOD.
Pearl has been used for centuries as a beautifying antioxidant and potent source of enzymes, biocompatible minerals, and amino acids. This adaptogen delivers dozens of essential trace minerals into the bloodstream for bone and cell building, longevity, joy, and overall glow.

PROBIOTICS

BEAUTY FOOD. DIGESTIVE AID. IMMUNITY FOOD.
Probiotics nurture intestinal microflora, heal the gut, cleanse the liver, and recolonize intestines with organisms that defend against disease, viruses, and yeast. Probiotics also enhance nutrient potency and assimilation, and decrease sugar cravings. When your microbiome is healthy, you will be rewarded with smoother digestion, increased energy, elevated mood, glowing skin, and stronger immunity.

REISHI

ADAPTOGEN. BRAIN ACTIVATOR. IMMUNITY FOOD.
Reishi mushroom is the strongest immune-boosting herb in the world, legendary for nourishing the heart and energizing the spirit. Our reishi relieves stress and imparts feelings of centeredness and strength, soothing allergies

and inflammation, protecting the liver, and supporting the brain.

SCHISANDRA BERRY

ADAPTOGEN. HORMONE BALANCER. BEAUTY FOOD.
Ground schisandra berry tonifies and heals all organs. It's legendary for increasing sexual function and bringing suppleness to the skin and shine to hair. Schisandra supports the liver, enhances stamina, counters stress, and heightens concentration.

TOCOTRIENOLS

BEAUTY FOOD. INFLAMMATION TAMER. DETOXIFIER.
This luxurious and creamy powder, derived from organic California rice, is a superconcentrated source of vitamins E, D, and antioxidants. It has tissue-regenerating, inflammation-taming, immunity-supporting, muscle-boosting, and toxin-removing powers that directly reach the brain, liver, heart, lungs, and kidneys.

FATS

CHIA SEEDS

ENERGY FOOD. DIGESTIVE AID. BRAIN ACTIVATOR.
Chia is a nutritional treasure chest, used for centuries as a potent source of omega-3 fatty acids, protein, fiber, antioxidants, and minerals. Chia seeds detoxify the body, clear the digestive system, stimulate the brain, and nourish the skin, hair, and internal organs. Feel the glow of this high-functioning brain and body fuel.

COCONUT MEAT & OIL

BEAUTY FOOD. BRAIN ACTIVATOR. METABOLISM BOOSTER.
Coconut supports the thyroid, balances blood sugar, boosts metabolism, and helps to eliminate toxins. Coconut is also strong immune fuel, alleviating adrenal stress and serving as an antiviral, antifungal, and antimicrobial agent. It improves digestion and the absorption of vitamins and amino acids, calcium, and magnesium.

HEMP SEEDS

ENERGY FOOD. BRAIN ACTIVATOR. IMMUNITY FOOD.
Hemp seeds are a potent source of plant protein and omega-3 essential fatty acids. These nutrients boost the immune system, act as anti-inflammatory agents, flush toxins, and help eliminate excess fat. Bursting with major and trace minerals, hemp seeds feed the brain, nourish the eyes, stimulate blood cells, and beautify hair and skin. Their complex, nutty flavor complements both savory and sweet foods.

NUTS & SEEDS

ENERGY FOOD. MINERALIZES DEEPLY. INFLAMMATION TAMER.
Omega-3 fatty acids and omega-6s are crucial for metabolism, brain function, mental health, cardiovascular health, and inflammatory response. My favorites are activated almonds, cashews, hemp seeds, pumpkin seeds, Brazil nuts, flaxseeds, hazelnuts, walnuts, macadamia nuts, and chia seeds.

ACCENTS

APPLE CIDER VINEGAR
This is one of the best tools in the kitchen. It's an alkalizing, energizing, cleansing, enzyme-potent, healing beauty food. I was a vinegar aficionado, traveling to distant towns just to collect their aged vinegars, but raw organic medicinal apple cider vinegar has single-handedly won me over, with its fresh and versatile flavor and the incredible ways in which it satiates my sour cravings while actually upgrading my body.

BLACK PEPPER
This warming, aromatic spice boosts the immune system, nourishes the kidneys, and activates digestion. My favorite way to use this spice is alongside meatier fruits like cherry, peach, and persimmon and in big pots of sweet milky teas flavored with cinnamon, ginger, and almond.

CARDAMOM
Cardamom is a whimsical, romantic spice that features prominently in thousands of years of culinary pleasure. An elegant pairing with many plant-based concoctions, it enhances the nuttiness of maca, the earthiness of medicinal herbs, and the depth of cacao. Cardamom is rich in minerals, and a stimulating aphrodisiac.

CAYENNE
Cayenne is a bioavailable metabolic stimulant, detoxifier, and circulatory activator. Its rich spice increases the pulse of lymphatic and digestive rhythms. Cayenne heats the body, aids digestion, and inspires enzyme production, supporting full-system cleansing and radiance.

CINNAMON
Cozy cinnamon is both fragrant and nourishing. Cinnamon effectively lowers blood sugar and tames inflammation, warming the palate and soothing the organs. Pair it with cacao, turmeric, cardamom, and mesquite powder.

MESQUITE
An ancient power food ground from a bean-like pod. Mesquite's malty caramel flavor is both decadent and low glycemic, aiding in sugar metabolism. It is dense in fiber, proteins, minerals, and the amino acid lysine, which produces collagen and antibodies.

NUTRITIONAL YEAST
Grown on molasses and dried into flakes, this magic powder gives a nutty, umami flavor to any dish, plus a B_{12} and complete protein boost.

PINK SALT
Himalayan pink salt is organic and raw, mined from pure, prehistoric seabeds. It works as an electrolyte, balancing fluid both within and outside your body's cell walls. Pink salt helps regulate pH, stimulate digestive enzymes, and transport amino acids into the bloodstream. Only sun-dried and never heated, Moon Juice pink salt contains trace minerals that detoxify, beautify, and balance from the inside out.

ROSE WATER
Consumed for centuries for health and beauty benefits, rose water is steam-distilled from organic roses. Add it to water, any hot or cold drink, dressing, or dessert for delicate sweetness. It can even be used as a facial mist with aloe and water to hydrate and soothe, for a dewy glow. It's cooling to the body, soothing to the heart and mind in stressful situations, an aphrodisiac, and supports metabolism and the digestive tract.

SEA VEGETABLES
Seaweed is extremely close to blood plasma in makeup and is rich in bioavailable iron, calcium, and iodine. These beautiful leaves from sea forests energize, boost metabolism, balance hormones, and nourish your blood and bones. They also happen to be some of the most

delicious elements of the plant kingdom. Just as each fish has its own unique flavor and texture, so do sea vegetables. They add an incredible umami element to dishes and range from sweet and mild to savory and salty, poignant marks of flavor and abundant tangles to fill bowls. I always have dulse, hijiki, kelp, and kombu in the pantry.

TURMERIC

Warming and fragrant, this potent root invigorates and cleanses the blood and liver in either powder form or fresh out of the ground. It's an incredible anti-inflammatory with pain-killing properties you can feel within thirty minutes. Turmeric also strengthens joints and tendons, is an antibacterial and antiseptic, helps your body digest fats, and even treats depression.

VANILLA

Moon Juice's raw ground vanilla comes from whole, hand-harvested, sun-dried beans. This potent and aromatic delicacy is an ancient aphrodisiac, soothing the nervous system and alleviating stress, while also acting as an antioxidant.

SWEETENERS

COCONUT NECTAR

Coconut nectar is an low glycemic sweetener (GI 35, compared to sugar's GI 68), so no crashing. The nectar is hand harvested as sap from the sugar blossoms that grow in the canopies of Indonesian coconut groves. Coconut nectar is high in potassium, iron, zinc, and B and C vitamins. We prefer it to agave because the unprocessed hand-collected floral sap from the blossoms of the coconut tree is enzymatically alive, mineralizing, and neutral in taste. Use it as you would honey.

DATES

The date is a dynamic sweetener that is packed with essential nutrients: calcium, amino acids, and iron to name only a few plus plenty of fiber. Their twenty different amino acids assist in digestion, and also furnish the body with energy. Dates are rich in vitamins, minerals, and fiber. Their dense, caramel sweetness enriches flavor profiles with depth. Soak them to soften and to incorporate more easily into milks or other recipes.

HONEY

Honey is a very healing food—it's medicine, a nutrient source, and a sweetener. In its organic raw form it is the richest source of healing enzymes, and contains minerals, antioxidants, and probiotics. It has antifungal, antiviral, and antibiotic effects and when taken with other mineral-rich foods will increase the body's mineral absorption.

STEVIA

We use the liquid extract of whole leaf stevia when a zero-glycemic sweetener is desired. It has been used for centuries in South America to aid diabetics and hypoglycemics.

YACÓN

Related to Jerusalem artichoke, yacón is a root whose raw syrup has a beautiful caramel flavor. It is low glycemic and contains prebiotic fiber that stimulates and supports the growth and activity of friendly probiotic bacteria that colonize your gut.

CHAPTER 2

RETHINK YOUR KITCHEN PRACTICE

As the plant-based food movement gains momentum, people everywhere are trying to figure out how to make impactful changes to their diets and lifestyles that are truly sustainable, exploring the health food store or the raw food aisle of their markets in increasing numbers. This book will help you jump into that movement to whatever degree works for you, whether you simply want to experiment with a few recipes that appeal to you or you want to start with two or three recipes that feed and build on one another—say, almond milk, an all-purpose pastry dough made from the resulting nut flour, and a nut cheese—and see how these methods can be easily integrated into your existing kitchen practice. Before long, you'll see how this food and this holistic approach to food preparation will completely transform your kitchen, the way you shop, and how you participate in the ecosystem that is our food chain.

The recipes in this book are intended to provide you with a solid understanding of how the ingredients we use at Moon Juice work and how you can most easily incorporate our principles into your own kitchen. After years of working in kitchens and now living as a working single mom, I've learned to prepare food efficiently. I look at my small kitchen as a business that has to run at least five days a week. I'm running a potent, high-vibe operation. All that's required are a few big-batch food projects throughout the year, some easy weekly prep, and a willingness to expand your experience of food. This book is filled with savvy tricks to help you bust it out.

Best of all, once you are in the groove of keeping your shelves and refrigerator stocked with the basic building blocks you'll learn to make in this book, you're never more than a minute or two away from a quick, satisfying, beautiful meal. If you do the heavy lifting of fermenting and sprouting and milling when you have more time, you can reap the benefits all week long. All that is required to assemble the perfect bite is the dollop of a spoon and the spread of a knife.

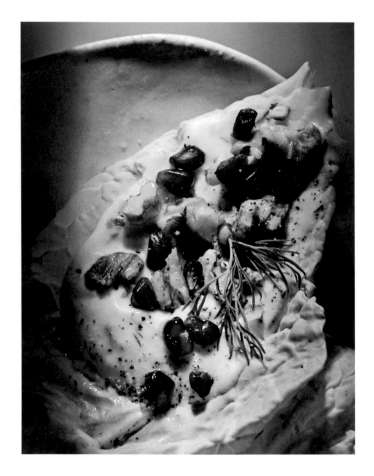

BE LAZY FANCY

Mixing and matching different pre-made components will allow you to throw together a gorgeous parfait-style Moon Pot, roll up a platter of savory wraps, or assemble a stunning layer cake at a moment's notice. It's an approach to cooking and entertaining that I call "lazy fancy," because it's hard to believe food so elegant can come together with so little effort. You'll see sug-

RAW FOODS TO KEEP ON HAND

Raw foods are mainstays of the Moon Kitchen. They are nutrient dense, versatile, delicious, easily available, and form the basis of simple snacks and meals that require only a few minutes of preparation. As you fall in love with these foods, the way they taste, and the way they make you feel, you will also fall in love with how easy meal prep becomes. You should feel free to pair these raw staples with whatever you like and have on hand, cooked or raw. For example, you can wrap a nori sheet around a baked sweet potato or steamed quinoa mixed with some cultured veggies and a handful of arugula. In one tidy package, you'll get raw seaweed, cultured veggies, and raw greens. I have always found that the more raw foods you incorporate in your diet, the more raw foods you will crave.

FERMENTED VEGETABLES

These vegetables are among the best foods you can eat, supplying the enzymes and probiotics that build immunity, improve digestion and nutrient absorption, create glowing skin, and improve mood. I eat them at least once a day, either straight out of the jar or on a raw cracker, in a salad, in a wrap, atop a soup, or in a bowl.

NORI

Nori is one of the most easily assimilated sources of minerals, and an awesome way to get iron, calcium, and iodine. Nori is a detoxifier, alkalizer, lymphatic cleanser, and liver and thyroid supporter. Think of nori as your new toast, wrap, or taco shell and fill it with more raw food, like avocado, shaved veggies and herbs, miso paste, spiced nut blends, and greens.

CACAO

Raw cacao is rich in minerals, happy-making chemicals for your brain, and antioxidants. It is extremely energizing, joy promoting, and stress relieving. Making chocolate is some of the most fun I have with raw food, adding medicinal herbs, superfoods, flowers, and fruit. I also love a chocolate malt nut milk shake in the morning. I make my chocolate with an organic stevia and coconut oil so I get all the minerals, antioxidants, good fat, energy, and hormone support without the glycemic hit.

AVOCADOS

An incredible source of good fats that feeds the brain, nervous system, and hormone production. They are perhaps the most versatile and crowd-pleasing raw food of all. I keep peeled avocado halves in my freezer and add them to smoothies instead of banana.

CASHEWS

Loaded with minerals and good fats, these nuts are particularly great for the brain, skin, bones, and mental health. For some creamy decadence, replace virtually any dairy product with blended cashews. Cashew milk is so creamy you don't need to strain it. Soaking them overnight before using them makes the nuts easier to assimilate into the body and washes away the acid that can leave you feeling bloated. If I am going to roll the activated nuts right into a recipe like milk, cheese, dressing, or ice cream, I rinse them and send them to the blender; otherwise, I dehydrate them and put them in the pantry.

GREEN LEAVES

My fridge is always filled with fresh herbs like basil, parsley, and cilantro. The key to success here is having them washed and on hand in abundance to throw raw into anything I make, from soup to fruit salads. I use arugula almost as Italians do pasta: It's a base for sauces, a bed for fermented vegetables, a stand-in for grains.

gestions throughout the book for Lazy Fancy combos to assemble from the Moon Foods you've made plus fresh ingredients or even store-bought elements.

To make any of the recipes in this book you don't need superior knife skills or a tricked-out kitchen, just an appreciation for simple, pure ingredients and a mind open to food's potential to change your outlook, energy, and fundamental health. As you begin to play and experiment with the recipes in this book, keep these principles in mind:

REVERE YOUR FOOD

One of the ways we can make whole, raw food a beautiful constant is to become ritualistic about the ingredients we use. Making a kitchen altar is an inexpensive, fun way to sensualize your journey into the Moon Kitchen, tease the alchemist out of you, and create new pathways to pleasure. Build an intentional space that could include wood, a gold spoon, talismans, objects from nature, special plates—anything that feels beautiful and sacred to you. Add some herbs you want to incorporate into your daily diet, a seasonal plant, or a pantry staple you made and want to experiment with. The space may be a portion of your counter, a designated fruit bowl, or the shelf above your blender. A kitchen altar brings a sense of reverence to food preparation that can turn mindless snacking into a moment of graciously hosting ourselves and toasting to health and beauty.

DON'T FAST, FEAST

To keep your metabolism going, your organs well supported, and your brain active, you must be fully fed and functioning. Treating yourself to an abundance of juice, milk, activated nuts and seeds, fruits, fermented foods, and vegetables is the ultimate indulgence, a holiday for the body. Foods from the Moon Kitchen are cleansing and enable the body to detox naturally and without deprivation while flooding it with nutrients and enzymes.

REFLECT WHAT YOU ABSORB

We are made of thought, light, food, feelings, and fluid. What you cultivate on the inside will begin to reverberate to your outside and will then be reflected back onto you through life's charm—the charm that comes from a life lived by someone who is thriving at the very core. Regularly eating good foods that feed the brain, hormones, and energy will radically enhance your mood and mental capacity, deeply affecting relationships and performance.

Lastly, as you prepare meals, get in the habit of tasting your food as you go. Each step along the way is a point at which you can adjust to variances in ingredients and personal desires for unique flavor and texture.

BREAK IT DOWN AND STOCK UP

Learning a few recipes is not going to radically change the way your mind organizes your kitchen and meals.

To truly inhabit the Moon Kitchen on an ongoing basis, you need to adopt an organized system of big-batch production and make it a home ritual. Nobody wants to soak and dehydrate for twenty-four hours, and then make the recipe à la minute. When you stock up on ingredients and pantry items like fresh yoghurt, cheese, cultured veggies, and other items you can mix and match to make nearly instant meals, you will be poised to cook spontaneously from this book and your imagination. Each day you will reach into your pantry, blending herbs and pantry foods into nut milks à la minute; building open-faced crisp sandwiches, bowls, broths, and wraps with your premade Moon Foods plus some fresh herbs and sliced veggies; maybe dipping a thing or two into a warmed premade chocolate; and, of course, creating anything else your inspired alchemist's heart desires.

The key to this microflow is making sure you're in a macro kitchen flow. This means making big batches of some provisions quarterly, tackling a fun recipe project each month, setting aside a day each week to do some light prep, and keeping your refrigerator stocked with lettuces, herbs, bowls of fruits, avocados, and squash, and the pantry stocked with your cosmic provisions, adaptogenic herbs, nuts, and seeds. It actually makes high-functioning eating so simple and practical that I wonder how I ever managed cooking most of my meals before I got down with this concise system.

I usually take forty-five minutes on Sunday mornings to set myself up for the week ahead. This includes preparing milks and dehydrating their pulps to make activated flour for future recipes; making yoghurts, kefir, and a hummus or puree; washing leaves for wraps; and starting a broth. I find the slicing, cleaning, and blending to be supremely relaxing;

BIG-BATCH PRODUCTION

In updating your kitchen practice the prospect of new rhythms may be intimidating but there are ways to maximize your potential in the kitchen by organizing your time. Each recipe in this book can be categorized as a recipe to make once a month, once a week, or daily. By keeping a rotation of these foods on hand you will effortlessly be in the Moon's Kitchen flow.

ONCE A QUARTER

Foods to line the pantry shelves: nut and seed mixes, crisps, dried fruits and vegetables, cultured vegetables, granolas, big-batch cosmic provisions; activating and milling your nuts and seeds; frosting bases and doughs to stock the freezer.

ONCE A WEEK

These provisions are best eaten fresh, and must be replenished on a weekly basis: nut and seed milks, yogurts, kefir. Pull out the frosting base to color and flavor; defrost a dough to make cookies, a tart, or cake; doll up your cheese with fresh herbs and shallots.

ONCE A MONTH

Nut cheese bases; jams, cookies and doughs, pickles. Divide into manageable postions and freeze if appropriate.

BI-WEEKLY OR DAILY

Juices. These will last no more a day or two, depending on the type of juicer you own (see page 56).

it's a moving meditation, a time to unplug from thoughts and phones. The mind goes quiet and slips into the rhythm of your moving hands, in awe of the perfect plant medicines you are touching.

Storage is the key to this operation: It's critical to have enough room and the right containers to store all you make. Rather than putting 8 quarts of nuts in one container, divide a large batch among several smaller, airtight containers so you can prevent unnecessary exposure to moisture, which takes away the crunchiness you worked to achieve in the dehydrator.

All the foods listed under big-batch production are perfect to stock your kitchen with and accommodate the fresh raw produce like greens, herbs, and fruits you buy each week. Ultimately, I'm confident you'll discover that blocking out the time to fill your pantry with Moon Kitchen staples and using them, plus a lot of live food, as the core of your diet is far *easier* than cooking meals from scratch every day.

THE WASTE-FREE KITCHEN

A lot of the recipes we use at Moon Juice were created out of necessity, a factor that drives creativity in most professional kitchens. Whatever that need may be—whether seasonal availability, budget or health concerns, or simply my own reluctance to throw out the by-products of other recipes—it's important to me that every part of our ingredients is put to use.

Throughout the book, you'll notice that I provide insights into how to use every part of what you bring into the kitchen. You may start to feel like your kitchen is alive.

When you are in full swing, you should have the constant hum of the dehydrator dehydrating pulp from the nut milks you made earlier in the day. You should have kefirs, a jar of raw chocolate, and sprouted nuts on your countertop. Your fridge will be filled with jams, juices, yoghurts, cheeses, and cultured veggies. Your pantry will be stocked with cakes, crisps, and snacks.

When I am in action like this, my kitchen feels like a science lab, a pharmacy, and my favorite bakery all at once. When I walk into the kitchen, I feel proud, nourished, and cared for. I'm always excited to check in on my little babies, to see how the dehydrator is doing, to dip my tasting spoon into one of the many fermentations happening inside and outside the fridge. The ceremonies and rituals you begin to develop with these foods are some of the many ways they will bring you joy.

ACTIVATING NUTS & SEEDS

It's always preferable to use activated nuts and seeds for the recipes in this book. Activating nuts, seeds, grains, and legumes is a very simple process and the most effective way to access all the nutrients in these living foods. Raw nuts contain phytic acid and enzyme inhibitors that reduce the body's ability to absorb certain nutrients properly. Soaking and rinsing removes enzyme inhibitors and allows the germination process to begin. It also allows the proteins to break down into separate amino acids, and the complex starches to break down into simpler carbohydrates, making them much easier to digest, as well as breaking down the problematic compounds of natural chemicals that can put pressure on your digestion or cause bloating.

As it activates, the plant's nutrient content multiplies, resulting in a fiber-rich food packed with higher levels of vitamins and minerals. Activated nuts and seeds can be stored in the refrigerator for a few days or dehydrated for longer storage. You may sometimes notice raw foods labeled "sprouted"; we use the term "activated" because in this process you are not truly bringing the nut or seed to a sprouted state where you see the green sprout emerge.

Activating nuts and seeds simply entails soaking them in water and pink salt for several hours to start the germination or sprouting process. For every 2 cups nuts or seeds, add 1 teaspoon pink salt and enough water (I prefer to use alkaline water) to cover. Leave them to soak for 7 to 12 hours (almonds need between 12 and 14 hours). If you won't be using the activated nuts or seeds within 72 hours, place them in a dehydrator for 12 to 24 hours, until completely dried (if they are not fully dry, they can become moldy). Stored in an airtight container, they will keep for 6 months or more.

DEHYDRATING AND MILLING FLOURS

You will notice that all the recipes calling for flours in the book specify activated flour, which means they were made from nuts, grains, or seeds that have been soaked. Ground nut pulp is the inevitable by-product of making nondairy milks at home, and an invaluable ingredient in the Moon Kitchen. Flours can be made from the pulps left over from creating any of the nut and seed milks. The pulp can be used as is in treats like Pulp Brownies (page 231) and other sweet or savory treats, but to expand its possibilities (and shelf life) infinitely, you can dehydrate the ground nuts and mill the result to create an activated flour. Simply spread the ground nuts on a dehydrator sheet and dehydrate until bone dry, about 12 hours, depending on your dehydrator; for a larger amount this can take even longer. A few tablespoons, spread thinly on the sheet, will dry much more quickly. Then transfer the ground nuts to a blender or food processor and grind until milled to a fine powder. Once you get into a habit of making your own Well Milks, you will always have a good supply of activated flour on hand. Store activated flours in an airtight container in a cool spot.

Nut and seed fats are energizing! They nourish body tissue and the brain, and deliver micronutrition and vital energy.

NUTS

USED IN

ALMONDS	Moon Milks; Dulse & Vinegar Almonds; Herb & Cheese crisps; pastry dough
HAZELNUTS	Moon Milks; Hazelnut Crunchers; Hazelnut Mesquite Streusel
WALNUTS	Moon Milks, Maca Mesquite Walnuts
BRAZIL NUTS	Moon Milks
CASHEWS	Cashew Butter Crème, Cheeses

SEEDS

USED IN

PUMPKIN SEEDS	Moon Milks; Turmeric, Coconut & Lime Pepitas; Salted Maple Reishi Granola; all crackers
SESAME SEEDS	Moon Milks, Chocolate Chaga Donuts
CHIA SEEDS	Chia Pudding, all crackers, Cumin & Chard Crisps, Fermented Green Crisps, jams, Carrot Gingerbread, Chocolate Chaga Donuts
SUNFLOWER SEEDS	All crackers, Fermented Green Crisps, Chocolate Chaga Donuts
FLAX SEEDS	All crackers, Fermented Green Crisps, Chocolate Chaga Donuts
BUCKWHEAT	Salted Maple Reishi Granola

EQUIPMENT

After years of working in a commercial kitchen, I realized that I could make just about anything with a sharp knife and a cast-iron pan. Years later I still take a minimalist approach to cooking, which is why you'll need only a few essential tools to reproduce all the recipes in this book.

ONE (BIG) SHARP KNIFE

A well-honed blade is the backbone of your culinary practice.

With this knife, you can do anything from cutting into large pumpkins to peeling the daintiest heirloom garlic. I'm a fan of the one-knife kitchen, and advocate for having almost religious respect for your knife's edge. People with less experience in the kitchen often prefer to use a smaller knife that may not be as sharp, but success and confidence will actually come from a large chef's knife that you keep sharp as a razor.

Sharpening your knife at the perfect angle is a meditative process. Start with a Japanese whetstone that has been soaked overnight (I never use the European metal grinding technique). To find the perfect angle, put a penny on the whetstone and place the knife on top. That angle is your sweet spot. Now move the knife down and across the stone, bringing the entire blade in contact with the stone as you go. Repeat until the blade is razor sharp and straight. Turn the blade over and repeat on the other side. When you put that much attention to personally shaping your knife, it becomes uniquely your own.

MANDOLINE

The mandoline is a great tool for anyone who consumes large amounts of plants on a daily basis. A good mandoline will minimize your prep time and allow you to thinly slice, shave, and grate vegetables into uniform, elegant pieces.

JUICER

At Moon Juice, we use a huge hydraulic juice press, but if you're not making juice for thousands of people a day, there are several types of juicers that are appropriate for home use. Each has distinct advantages and disadvantages—and different price points.

PRESS JUICER This juicer gets the job done by extracting with a lot of pressure. Squeezing the juice out of leaves, roots, veggies, and fruits between two plates breaks the cell walls naturally and without lots of oxidation, retaining the most nutrients drop for drop. Pressed juice also has the longest shelf life, up to 72 hours, so you can make juice a couple times per week rather than several times per day. It's by far the biggest investment, but if you drink a lot of juice daily, the investment will pay off over the years.

MASTICATING JUICER This middle-ground juicer typically has a horizontal design. The fruits and vegetables are pushed into a tube where they are crushed and squeezed and juice is drained. This machine has great juice yields and retains most of the nutrients. It's great at juicing greens and herbs, and works at lower speeds with less oxidation to make juice with a shelf life of around 48 hours.

TWIN-GEAR JUICER I used this kind of machine for years. It results in a wonderful, nutrient-dense juice and costs a fraction of what a press juicer will run you. Its two interlocking gears work at slow speeds to extract the juice, resulting in less oxidation and undamaged nutrients, so the juice has a longer shelf life

(72 hours). The method extracts most of the juice, enzymes, vitamins, and minerals from your plant material. The limitation with this machine is speed; if you are willing to hand-feed every leaf into the machine, and clean each part of the juicer with a toothbrush after each use, this is the winner.

CENTRIFUGAL JUICER This is the machine you'll find in most juice bars. Food is pushed into a rapidly spinning mesh chamber with sharp teeth on its floor, using centrifugal force to fling the juice away from the pulp. This is a very user-friendly machine and has a low buy-in, so it's the perfect machine for someone wanting to test the waters of home juicing. Centrifugal juicers work best with soft and hard fruits and vegetables, but less well with leafy greens and herbs. The centrifugal action oxidizes the juice, though, so ideally you'll want to drink this juice within 10 minutes of making it.

BLENDER BOTTLE

This is one of my favorite tools, and it also happens to cost less than $10. An oversized beverage container with a screw-on lid, drinking spout, and a whisk-like metal sphere to agitate the contents when shaken, this will proficiently blend power foods like adaptogens and proteins with any liquid. I carry mine around daily to enjoy homemade Moon Milks spiked with protein and adaptogens on the go.

DEHYDRATOR

Think of dehydrating as slow baking, using the element of air as you would use the elements of fire and water to take food preparation to the next level. I recommend a home dehydrator that can sit on your counter as a microwave might. It's the little "oven" that will "cook" you through a good deal of this book.

You can buy a dehydrator with as few as two trays or as many as nine. With a larger one, you can dehydrate several things at once or incubate ferments, cheeses, yoghurts, and veggies

to control fermentation. You can also use a dehydrator to warm cakes, cookies, and breads made from raw ingredients without "cooking" them. In general, the recipes in this book are dehydrated at a temperature of about 118°F, which may translate to the "live food" setting if your dehydrator doesn't indicate temperature. You should always consider dehydrating times approximate, as the temperature of your machine, the temperature of your kitchen, and humidity can all affect how long your foods will need to dehydrate. My best advice is to check the food frequently until you get to know your machine.

Keeping the dehydrator on your counter will encourage you to prolong the lives of things like ripe, seasonal fruit, the harvest of an abundant herb patch, teas, bread, cookies and crackers made from pulp, and your own creations that the techniques in this book will inspire.

Dehydrators are super forgiving, and it's safe to leave them running 24/7. You can throw something in to test for fun and run off to work. Nothing will burn, and you can often "rehydrate" an overdried trial with water if need be.

NONSTICK BAKING MATS

These flexible silicone baking mats are the surfaces on which you will create dehydrated treats, flours, and provisions. As a "baking" surface, they will give you the ease and freedom to make large batches of a recipe or single ingredients, allowing you to reshape and flip your ingredients after you transfer them from the bowl or blender.

HIGH-SPEED BLENDER

I'm not one for expensive gadgets, but this is an investment I urge you to consider. The amount of air these powerful blenders can whip into ingredients completely transforms them, quickly breaking them down and incorporating air to deliver unparalleled mouthfeel and texture.

I use my high-speed blender to make nut and seed milks, smoothies, shakes, puddings, soups, flours, ice creams, and medicinal blends throughout the day. As you incorporate high-functioning foods into your life, a high-power blender will truly be a life-changing tool.

That said, the recipes in this book can be made in a regular blender. It may just take a bit longer and the final result will not be as silky smooth, but it will still be delicious.

NUT MILK BAG/CHEESECLOTH

The fine mesh of a nut milk bag or cheesecloth is ideal for separating nut and seed solids from their liquid. Nut milk bags are wonderful because they can be washed and reused, but if you don't have one yet, cheesecloth or even a (clean) thin cotton T-shirt can serve as an in-a-pinch alternative. You can purchase cheesecloth at many supermarkets and specialty cookware stores, and a nut milk bag at your local health food store. If you can't find a nut milk bag, purchase a paint bag from the hardware store.

BROTH POT

Once you're in broth mode, you want to make sure your pot is large enough to match your intentions. I suggest one with a capacity of at least 6 gallons.

FERMENTING JAR

A German ceramic crock is the ideal (and most picturesque) environment in which to ferment vegetables, but I've been quite successful using a 1-quart or 6-cup wide-mouth jar with a screw or clamp top. I like to go big so I can eat often, making large batches in a 1-gallon jar, but start as small as you want.

STORAGE CONTAINERS

Wide-mouth glass containers with removable lids can be purchased in sets, and are your best allies for storing your dehydrated goods. If you leave them exposed to the environment, your crackers, granolas, nut and seed crunchers,

and cookies will act as sponges and reabsorb the moisture in the air, losing their baked-to-perfection crispness. Airtight containers will keep the moisture out and maintain your treats' proper textures.

Once you've geared up to make quarterly batches of your favorite Moon Foods, you should consider investing in a small vacuum sealer. They're cheaper, smaller, and easier to use than you may think!

GO WITH THE FLOW

As you become more familiar with the recipes and ingredients in the Moon Kitchen, as well as my systems for simplifying, filling your pantry, and putting together meals, you will gain confidence and mastery over things that may initially seem too involved, too confusing. You will join the natural flow of these systems that I created from the strict *mise en place* training I received from French kitchens and the intuitive nature that takes place in making a home kitchen buzz, and continue on to your own discoveries. You'll quickly come to see that there is a method to the madness and a theory to the chaos. Once you begin making your own milks, you will automatically find yourself milling flour from the leftover nut pulp. (I suggest you keep your dehydrator right next to your blender so you can easily transfer the pulp onto the dehydrator trays.) You will soon have filled your pantry with flours ready to transform into breads, crisps, cakes, cookies, and cereals.

When you transform that flour into batches of dough you can store in the freezer, it becomes easy to whip out sweet or savory tarts, cookies, and protein bars that will utilize the large batches of cheese, jams, and chocolates you will be making from scratch. This truly is a holistic and sustainable system for the kitchen, in which every recipe builds on those you've already prepared. Once you find your groove, you'll have adopted an approach to food and cooking that will help feed you for a lifetime.

You will marvel at how self-sufficient you've become, and how by just bringing whole fruits, vegetables, seeds, and nuts into your home you can become your own market, stocking the shelves of your refrigerator and pantry with fresh milks, cheeses, yoghurt, freshly milled flours, doughs, crackers, jams, chocolate, and more. Think about the amount of packaging, shipping, and shopping you'll eliminate in a year by incorporating these practices! Watch your kitchen, your grocery basket, and your monthly bills change—along with your daily timeline for making dinner or dessert—as you experience profound internal changes.

COOK THE
MOON

MOON GUIDE

Throughout this book I have annotated each recipe with its most potent benefits. These are not comprehensive, and you may want to refer back to pages 39–41 for a key to the properties of the individual ingredients for the full list of benefits to be derived from a given recipe. When you combine components to make a layered parfait, wrap, sandwich, or assembled dessert, you are simply multiplying the powers of your food! However, if you are seeking specific benefits, these annotations will help you zero in on the recipes that will best address your concerns.

ALKALIZER
Foods and potions that help balance your body's pH, restoring harmony in your blood and internal organs.

APHRODISIAC
These foods and potions stimulate libido and awaken your body, heart, and mind's most sensual inclinations.

BEAUTY FOOD
These foods and potions promote glowing skin, eyes, and hair, stimulating cellular restoration, preservation, and longevity.

BRAIN ACTIVATOR
Provides necessary fatty acids and nutrients to feed your brain, enhancing memory, focus, and clarity.

DETOXIFIER
Foods or potions that cleanse the gut, organs, blood, and lymphatic system of toxic accumulations.

DIGESTIVE AID
Soothes digestion and tummy troubles, easing nausea and promoting intestinal health.

ENERGY FOOD
These foods and potions deliver a supercharged dose of sustainable energy for mental, physical, and spiritual vitality.

HORMONE BALANCER
Foods that support the glands that produce and regulate hormones, helping to balance mood, weight, and vitality. These adaptogens are generally mild but persistent and effective; they may be taken over long periods for overall health.

IMMUNITY FOOD
These foods and potions support your immune system by stimulating and supplementing your body's inherent germ- and virus-busting properties.

INFLAMMATION TAMER
These foods and potions decrease inflammation in joints, tissues, and organs, contributing to overall balance and longevity.

JOY PROMOTER
These are foods that elevate your mood and promote feel-good vibrations that entwine body, mind, and spirit.

LOW GLYCEMIC
These foods and potions contain less than 3 grams of sugar per serving, making them appropriate for a low-glycemic, low-sugar, or anti-candida diet.

METABOLISM BOOSTER
Metabolism is the process your body uses to convert food into energy, and these foods will up your metabolic rate for weight management and muscle retention.

MINERALIZES DEEPLY
The most effective way to get minerals is through plant sources that take inassimilable minerals found in the soil and ocean and put them into a form that the body can absorb and use. These foods sink into your body to build bone and tooth strength, nourish the skin and brain, calm the nerves, and balance acidity.

PLANT PROTEIN
These foods and potions feed muscles, tissues, and organs with essential amino acids and proteins for lasting energy, focus, and strength.

PROBIOTIC
Foods that deliver the good microbes into your gut, supporting your immune system, protecting you from disease, detoxifying your body, giving you glowing clear skin and white eyes, keeping you slim, and clearing brain fog.

STRESS RELIEVER
These foods and potions act as nerve tonics, soothing your nervous system and helping to restore your body and mind to their natural states of well-being.

THYROID SUPPORT
Foods that support the glands that produce and regulate hormones, helping to balance mood, weight, and vitality. These adaptogens are normally mild but persistent and effective; they may be taken over long periods for overall health.

CHAPTER 3

JUICES

I firmly believe we should be drinking unsweetened green juices—that is, those made without fruits like apples and pears or other high-glycemic ingredients such as beets and carrots—all day long.

Juicing alchemizes vegetables, fruits, and leaves into highly medicinal nectars capable of healing the body and mind. Juices are the most nutrient-dense fuel around, loaded with enzymes, vitamins, trace minerals, and other vital elements. Drinking these unsweetened juices is just about as close as you can get to mainlining raw, organic vegetables, herbs, and fruits. Juice is also deeply calming to the nervous system and full of nutrients that can easily be absorbed into the body without taxing the digestive system.

When I drink sweeter juices made with roots and fruits, I do so sparingly and for specific benefits: beets for the kidneys, carrots for fortifying the body, heavy doses of ginger and lemon with low-glycemic green apple for immunity, or melons in the summer for hydration. But the basis of my practice is a constant flow of green vegetables and leaves that alkalize and mineralize, and are incredible sources of bioavailable calcium and protein.

If you're using a slow juicer or press, you'll only need to prepare juices two or three times per week. With proper refrigeration, they will maintain their nutritional stability and taste crisp for 72 hours. If you're using a centrifugal juicer, though, it's important to juice daily for optimal benefit and nutrition, and to consume the juice within 10 minutes of making it. (See page 56 for more on choosing the right juicer for you.)

Most of these recipes yield about 20 ounces of juice, the equivalent of a large juice bar serving, or about 30 percent more than a typical bottled juice. Depending on your appetite, this will be one or two servings.

When preparing ingredients for juicing, discard any part of your fruits and veggies that look yellow, old, smushed, or tattered. Make sure all leaves are thoroughly—and properly—washed. Feel free to use the stems of leafy greens in your juice.

Note: When recipes call for chopped ingredients, it is primarily to give you a sense of volume. You need only chop ingredients into pieces small enough to fit into the tube of your juicer.

I DRINK A LOT OF GREEN JUICE—*a lot* of green juice—and this is my go-to. It's a formula I came up with many moons ago to keep up my energy during long nights working the line at a fine dining restaurant. Both practical and potent, it's a medicinal-grade juice that really exemplifies what plants can do for our bodies and minds. The blend is made without apples, and I encourage you to start training your palate to fall in love with the natural sweetness of spinach and parsley. I also love being able to mainline a potent dose of dandelion greens. Though our palates have gradually come to prefer white, soft, and sweet foods over bitter ones, bitter foods are invaluable for getting bile production going and cleansing the liver, and for supporting digestion and detoxification. I've found that opening my palate to the bitter side of the spectrum has, in time, led to new depths of sensory pleasure.

When I opened Moon Juice, I wondered if anyone would want to drink organic, all-green juice with heavy amounts of dandelion. To my great relief and joy, this has been our top seller since day one.

Goodness Greens acts like a blood transfusion. Chlorophyll, the biomolecule that makes this juice so green, looks almost identical to blood plasma under a microscope. Literal and visible evidence like this reaffirms my belief in how powerful this stuff is.

GOODNESS GREENS

ENERGY
FOOD

JOY
PROMOTER

DETOXIFIER

MAKES 20 OUNCES

10 celery stalks
1½ cups very tightly packed
   spinach
1 cup tightly packed kale
1 cup tightly packed fresh parsley
1 cup tightly packed dandelion
   leaves

Feed all the ingredients into a juicer, alternating the celery stalks with the greens and parsley. Stir and serve.

Note Celery leaves have an especially bitter taste, so you may want to remove them from the stalks until your palate has adjusted to their flavor. Reserve them for a broth or salad.

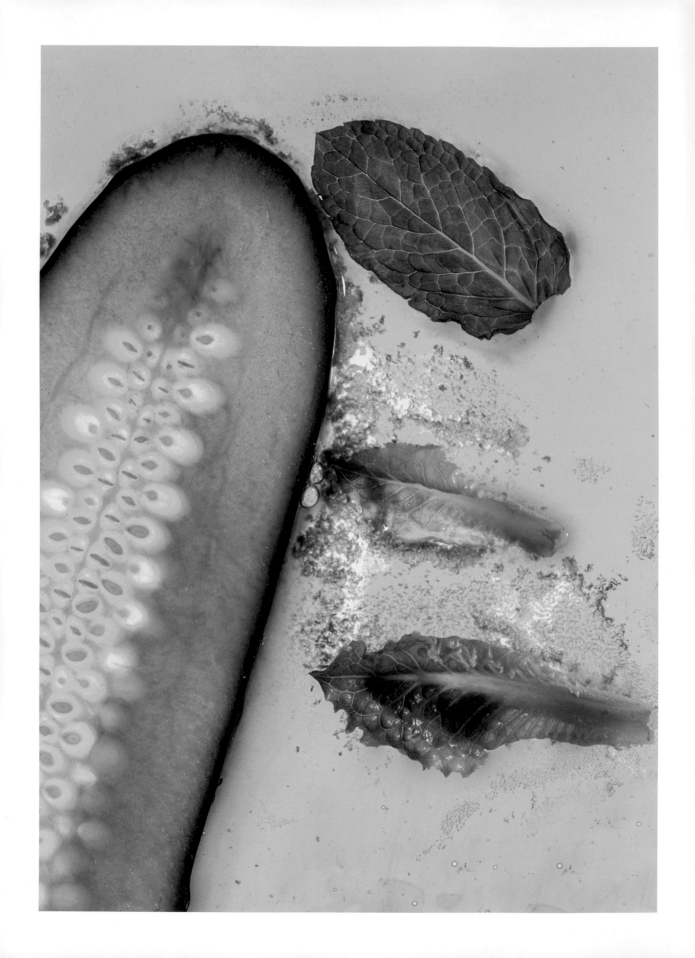

THE INHERENT SWEETNESS of spinach and cucumber are accented by the elegant, vegetal notes of mint and lettuce in this delicate blend. It's great for warmer weather or the days you don't want a heavy hitter with loads of bitter greens. Gracious Greens helps bestow glowing skin as it alkalizes and hydrates with cucumber, and cleanses, alkalizes, and deeply mineralizes with loads of spinach and mint. The lettuce specifically supports skin, hair, and nails.

ALKALIZER

BEAUTY
FOOD

DIGESTIVE
AID

GRACIOUS GREENS

MAKES 20 OUNCES

1 head romaine lettuce, root end
    trimmed
1½ to 2 European cucumbers
    or an equivalent weight of
    Kirby, Persian, or standard
    cucumbers
1 cup tightly packed spinach
15 sprigs mint
½ lemon (see Note)

Feed all the ingredients into a juicer, alternating the greens and herbs with the cucumbers. Stir and serve.

Note Unless you are using a centrifugal juicer, either remove the pith and peel from the lemon before juicing or squeeze the lemon by hand and stir in the juice to avoid releasing the bitterness of the peel into your juice.

THE RAINBOW CHARD IN THIS BLEND creates a magical color from its pink, red, and gold ribs. The deeply nourishing and grounding tone of this juice reminds me of the earth in the great canyons surrounding Los Angeles.

Containing bountiful collards and chard, this blend is high in calcium and iron, which deeply supports plant eaters' strength and stamina.

CANYON GREENS

MAKES 20 OUNCES

¾ cup tightly packed fresh parsley
1 (1-inch) piece fresh ginger
3 collard greens with ribs
4 rainbow chard leaves with ribs
1½ European cucumbers, or an
    equivalent weight of Kirby,
    Persian, or standard
    cucumbers
⅓ head celery (about 4 stalks),
    coarsely chopped

Feed all the ingredients into a juicer, alternating the additions as you go. Stir and serve.

ALKALIZER

IMMUNITY
FOOD

ENERGY
FOOD

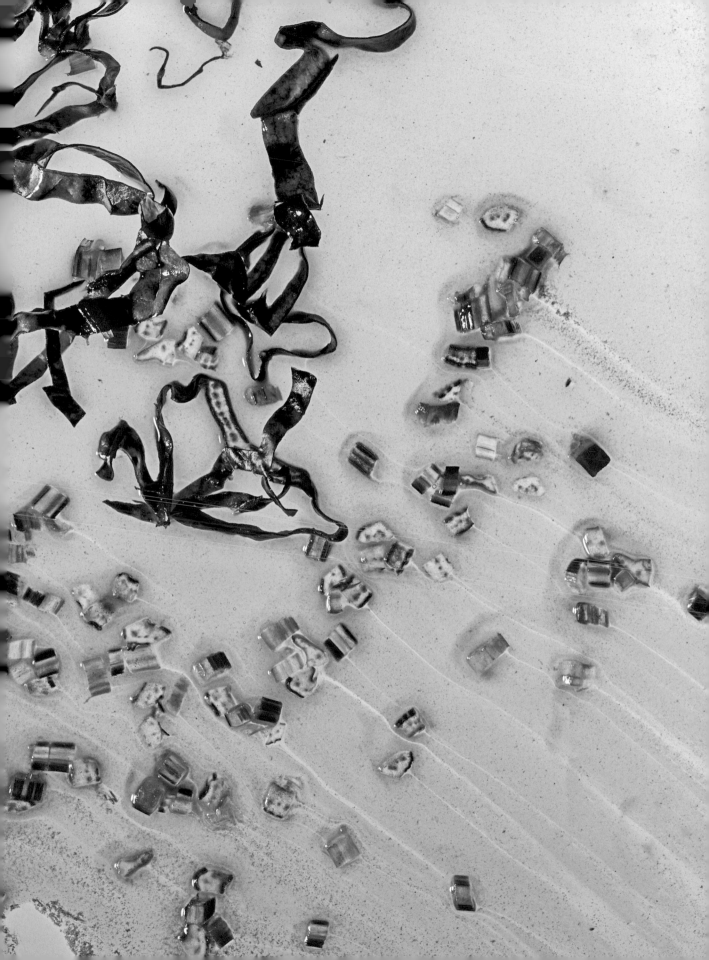

CILANTRO CELERY PUNCH is a cheerful name for a potent antidote to the heavy metals in our atmosphere. Every day we are bombarded with aluminum, barium, nickel, and cadmium, among many other chemicals. Cilantro and apple skins are among nature's only powerful heavy-metal cleansers. While this punch is working hard to cleanse your cells, you will be taken on a palate-cleansing and awesomely refreshing ride. The healthy dose of celery is deeply mineralizing and soothing to the nervous system.

Cilantro Celery Punch combines clean and slightly sweet flavors, setting the stage for cilantro's herbal elegance in perfect balance. In fact, many people who claim not to like cilantro end up guzzling this drink.

This is the juice to reward the conqueror—or just make you feel like one on a lazy day.

CILANTRO CELERY PUNCH

MAKES 20 OUNCES

DETOXIFIER

STRESS RELIEVER

INFLAMMATION TAMER

10 celery stalks, coarsely chopped (see Note)
2½ green apples, halved
1 (1-inch) piece fresh ginger
1½ cups tightly packed fresh cilantro
Juice of ½ lemon (see Note, page 73)

Feed the celery, apples, ginger, and cilantro into a juicer, alternating the herbs with the apples and celery. Stir in the lemon juice and serve.

Note Larger celery ribs will produce more juice than the inner leaves; the more leaves you include, the stronger and saltier your juice may be.

IN ITALY I FELL IN love with fennel and ate it raw and shaved, braised and grilled. I especially enjoyed its flavor in my favorite knock-your-socks-off-strength digestifs. After moving to Los Angeles, I was charmed by the sight of wild fennel growing off the freeway. I began foraging wild fennel growing in Malibu and used it to make my own medicinal tinctures and teas at home.

I initially recommended this blend to soothe the head, chest, and stomach while offering a journey into the aromatic wilds of California. A few weeks after having my son, Rohan, I was reminded of another of fennel's qualities: Within 20 minutes of drinking a tall glass of this juice, I was so engorged with breast milk that out of desperation I had to leave the kitchen and coax Rohan to nurse. When I shared that story with a few of our new mom Moon Juicers, Fennel Frond & Herb became a bit of an urban legend. I frequently have women stopping me on the street to tell me how this juice supported their family. While fennel is known to increase the flow of breast milk, its healing properties also pass into your milk to soothe your baby's stomach.

Even if you're not breast-feeding, fennel is a powerful treatment for bloating, indigestion, and respiratory distress. Fennel treats sinus congestion and coughs and is high in vitamin C, while basil eases headaches caused by tension and tight muscles.

FENNEL, FROND, & HERB

MAKES 20 OUNCES

DIGESTIVE AID

ALKALIZER

STRESS RELIEVER

1 fennel bulb with fronds (about 1 pound)
½ cucumber
1 green apple, halved
1½ cups lightly packed fresh basil

Trim the base off the fennel bulb to remove the root. Trim off and reserve the fronds. Cut the bulb and stalks into chunks that will fit into the juicer tube. Feed all the ingredients into a juicer, alternating the fennel bulb and stalks with the cucumber, apple, basil, and fennel fronds. Stir and serve.

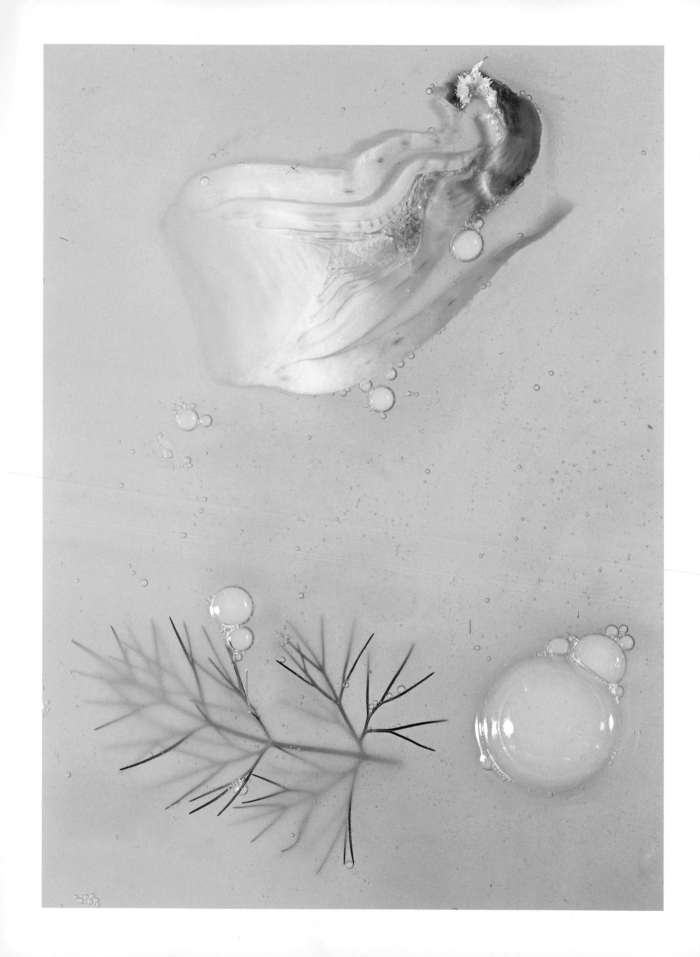

THIS JUICE IS THE PERFECT BALANCE of sour, sweet, and spicy. It's our best seller after Goodness Greens, a testament to my years of working in restaurant kitchens, where I learned to harmonize flavors so that just three ingredients deliver a symphony. It all comes down to an exact balance of elemental flavors.

Because it is so simple, this recipe will instantly allow you to observe how much flavor a particular ingredient yields. Switch up the variety of apple and notice how the acidity of the blend changes depending on the fruit and quantity you use.

GINGERED LEMON

MAKES 20 OUNCES

DETOXIFIER

DIGESTIVE AID

IMMUNITY FOOD

3 Granny Smith apples, halved
2½ lemons, halved (see Note, page 73)
1 (3-inch) piece fresh ginger

Feed all the ingredients into a juicer, alternating the additions as you go. Stir and serve.

VARIATION
For a Gingered Lemon Hot Toddy, stir in 1 teaspoon apple cider vinegar. Gently warm the mixture in a saucepan; just before bubbles start to appear, pour the toddy into a mug.

A LOT OF PEOPLE who don't like tomatoes are dubious about this, but you can't actually taste the tomato. It introduces an element of umami and evokes the carnal experience of biting into watermelon flesh that is lost when the fruit is juiced. The lime lets these two summer beauties sing.

Both watermelon and tomato are very high in lycopene, an antioxidant found in red fruits and veggies. I always tell members of my Moon Family—customers and employees alike—that this juice will incite rosy cheeks and boners. It's just that powerful at increasing blood flow. Save the watermelon rinds to make Minted Watermelon Rind with Aloe (page 85).

WATERMELON, TOMATO, LIME PUNCH

MAKES 20 OUNCES

APHRODISIAC

DETOXIFIER

ALKALIZER

2 pounds watermelon, rinds removed, flesh cut into big chunks

1 Roma or Early Girl tomato, chopped (about ¾ cup)

1 juicy lime (see Note, page 73)

Feed all the ingredients into a juicer, alternating between the melon and tomatoes. Stir and serve.

THIS JUST HAPPENS TO USE the exact amount of rind you'll have left over from making Watermelon, Tomato, Lime Punch (page 88). Choose organic aloe vera juice made from the raw, whole leaves, available at natural food and grocery stores.

MINTED WATERMELON RIND WITH ALOE

MAKES 20 OUNCES

BEAUTY
FOOD

ALKALIZER

DETOXIFIER

1½ cups coarsely chopped
    watermelon rind
½ cup lightly packed fresh mint
8 ounces fresh aloe vera juice

Feed the watermelon rind and mint into a juicer, alternating between them. Stir in the aloe juice and serve.

I **INCORPORATE** yams into my diet whenever I can, as they are incredible for short-term memory support and hormonal harmony. This blend is not too sweet—it's a deeply grounding, earthy concoction using just a touch of apple to bring these three golden roots out of the ground and into your glass.

My favorite element of the Spiced Yam is its almost chewy mouthfeel—radiant carrot juice teases out yam's every last milky mineral. Paired with ginger's spice and the aromatic oils of pressed cinnamon, this is a uniquely rich juice.

SPICED YAM

MAKES 20 OUNCES

4 sweet red apples, such as Red
  Delicious
5 cups coarsely chopped
  orange-fleshed sweet potatoes
  (about 6 small or 3 large)
1 pound carrots (8 thin medium
  carrots)
1 (2-inch) piece fresh ginger
¼ teaspoon ground cinnamon

Feed the apples, sweet potatoes, carrots, and ginger into a juicer, alternating among the ingredients. Stir in the cinnamon and serve.

HORMONE
BALANCER

BRAIN
ACTIVATOR

MINERALIZES
DEEPLY

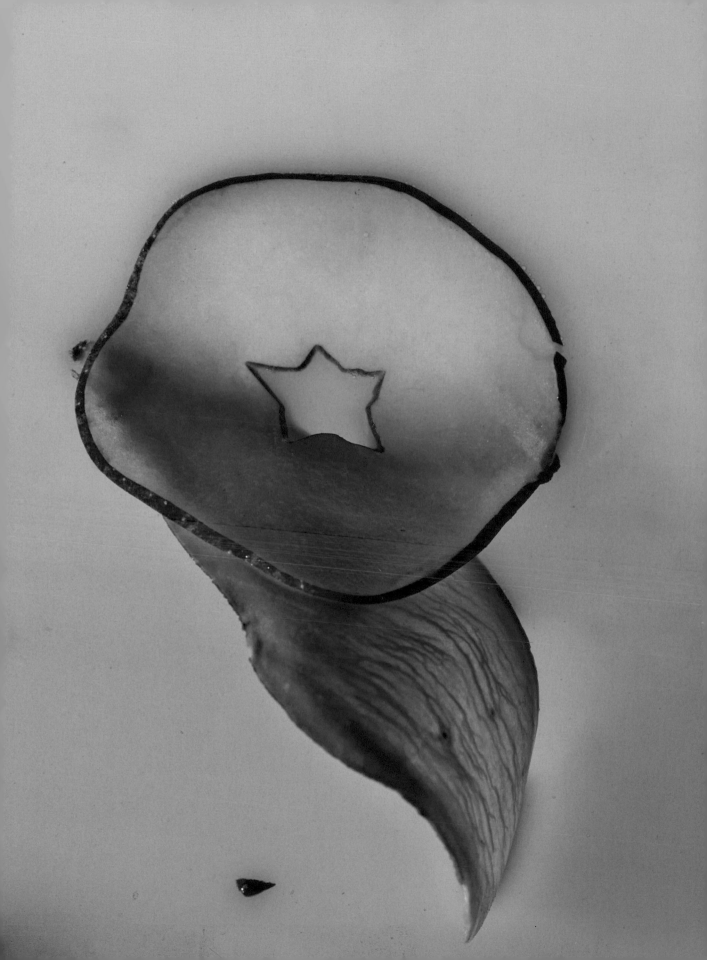

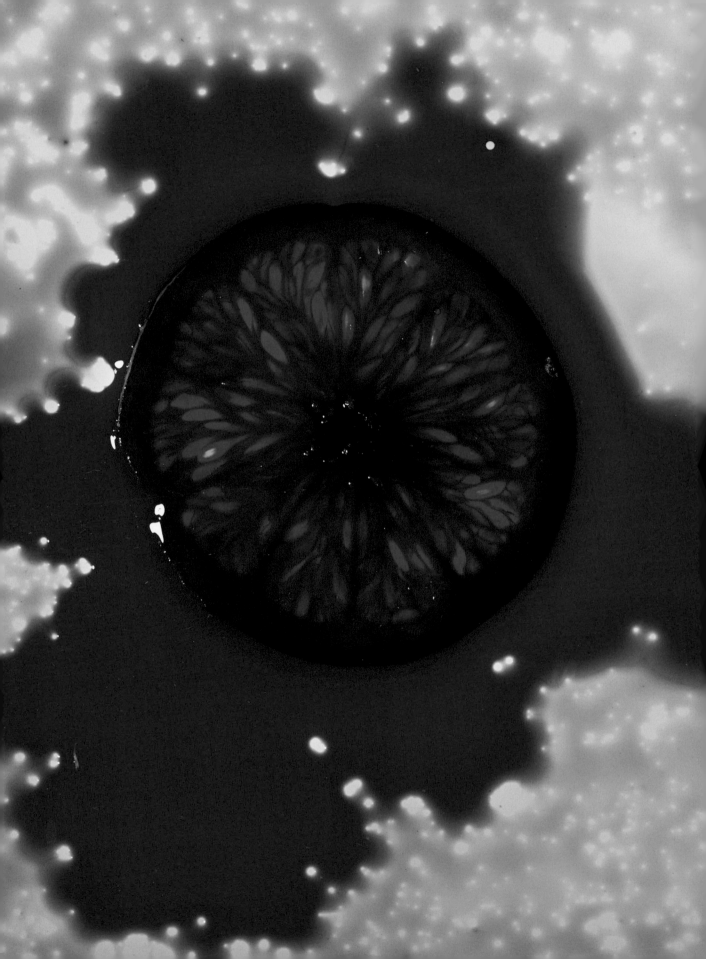

BEET AID is not your traditional beet juice. It's fresh, tart, and clean, unlike so many of the cloyingly sweet juice blends that commingle bright red beet juice with carrot and apple.

In the style of a Mexican limeade, Beet Aid celebrates beets' kidney-supporting and blood-nourishing properties using the root's own sweetness brightened by juicy limes and hydrating cucumber juice.

BEET AID

MAKES 20 OUNCES

ENERGY FOOD

DETOXIFIER

LOW GLYCEMIC

2 English or hothouse cucumbers
½ pound red beets
2 big juicy limes, or 6 tablespoons fresh lime juice (see Note, page 73)

Feed all the ingredients into a juicer, alternating among the ingredients. Stir and serve.

THE ENZYME IN RAW PINEAPPLE targets any type of inflammation, drastically aiding in cellular recovery and digestion, which explains why it's one of the few juices traditional Western doctors recommend for post-op consumption.

Bromelain, found in pineapple, effectively breaks down matter in the intestines, improving assimilation of nutrients and helping to achieve a clarity in the gut that will shine through your skin.

I've put enough pineapple in here for you to feel the effects of the bromelain; because it is also high in natural sugars, I've balanced the pineapple with cucumber, which alkalizes and lubricates the digestive tract in order to minimize excess sugar absorption. Jalapeño provides a metabolism-activating and blood-warming hit.

CUCUMBER PINEAPPLE JALAPEÑO

MAKES 20 OUNCES

DIGESTIVE AID

INFLAMMATION TAMER

METABOLISM BOOSTER

1 jalapeño, halved and seeded
2½ cups ripe pineapple
(about ⅕ of a peeled pineapple, or 20 ounces)
2 cups chopped cucumber
(1½ hothouse variety, or 12 ounces)

Feed all the ingredients into a juicer, alternating among the ingredients. Stir and serve.

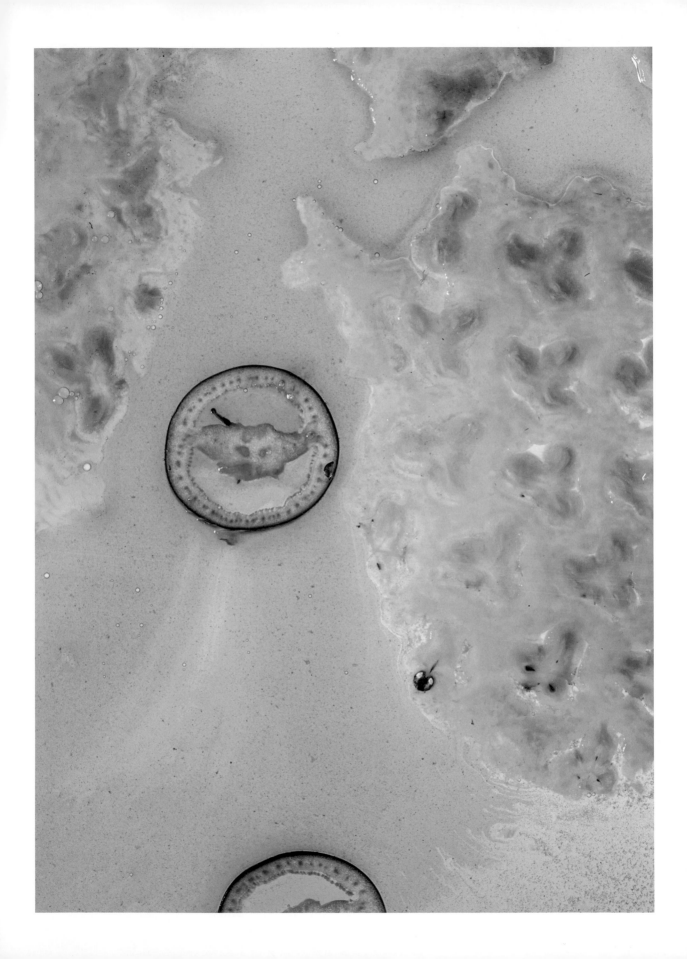

CHAPTER 4

WELL MILKS

Milks made from activated nuts and seeds are a gateway to a brighter life. These Well Milks are a great way to consume raw fats, minerals, and proteins and are less taxing digestively than consuming large amounts of raw nuts and seeds. The proteins these milks provide are valuable additions to a plant-based diet, and making them is insanely easy.

Activating nuts and seeds before they are blended into milks awakens their dormant energy. It also increases vitamins B and C, iron, calcium, and amino acid content, and heightens digestibility—all good reasons to begin activating your nuts and seeds in water you would want to drink, whether it is filtered, spring, or alkaline. (See page 53 for information on activating seeds and nuts.)

Other milks, like those made from hemp seeds or sesame seeds, are even easier to make in that they don't require soaking or straining. I call these Minute Milks, and they are the perfect option when you don't have the time to plan ahead.

These homemade Well Milks and Minute Milks are at the heart of many recipes in this book, and a core ingredient you will want to be creating weekly for your daily use. Use them in cereals, porridges, teas, soups, ice pops, and on their own as a perfect, fast-energizing plant protein. They are also the principal component of my Moon Milks and Moon Lattes. These luscious blends are decadently flavored superfuel, packed with high-functioning adaptogens and vitality-building plants to power your body and mind. Synergizing the milk of sprouted nuts and seeds with romantic spices, medicinal herbs, and low-glycemic sweeteners, Moon Milks and Lattes are deeply mineralizing, bone strengthening, and an amazing source of complete protein.

MAKING NUT & SEED MILKS

There's no need to go to the grocery store and buy a pasteurized nut milk when it's so simple to make delicious, decadent, activated milk at home. Fifteen minutes is all you need to make a weekly supply of your household "well milk" once you've developed an efficient system. Mastering this flow, from activating the nuts and seeds to blending and hand-pressing enough milk to get you through the bulk of the week and drying (and using) the resulting pulp is a ritual that will transform your life—and kitchen—experience.

I'm a purist, so for the most part my Well Milks are the simplest expressions of their primary ingredient. To experience each nut or seed's pure state and natural sweetness, try the milk unsweetened to begin with, then add sweetness to taste if needed.

Here's a round-up of nut and seed milks for you to experiment with, each offering different flavor profiles and medicinal qualities. If you love the flavors of vanilla, cardamom, and cinnamon, you can delicately accent your milks with a pinch of ground spice or vanilla beans.

Don't forget to make drying and milling your nut pulps part of your weekly kitchen practice (see page 54 for more on milling flours). If you are experimenting with making several different types of nut milks, don't be afraid to dehydrate handfuls of nut pulps and combine them to make a blended flour that you can really get cooking with.

WELL MILKS

Each Well Milk has its own distinctive characteristics and uses. Choose the one that best suits your tastes and purposes from the list below.

Our standard nut milk is a bit more luxurious than what you generally get from purchased milks, with a higher protein and fat content as well. Play with your own preference from week to week and application to application. On days when I will be eating less, for example, I make a heavier nut milk to deliver extra energy.

There's another unexpected bonus to making nut milk: There's

nothing like the foam that comes off freshly made nut milk. The delicate taste, texture, and aroma are ephemeral—you don't get them if you don't make your own.

Be careful not to overblend the nuts or the fragments will pass through the bag when you strain it and your milk will be grainy. Strain the liquid through a nut milk bag into a large bowl. Wring and squeeze the bag to get as much liquid from the nuts as possible; those last few drops will be the creamiest. Transfer the milk to an airtight container and refrigerate for up to five days. Store or dehydrate the nut pulp (see page 54) for other uses.

ALMOND MILK

Almonds are the nut that started it all—the gateway nut, if you will. The true beauty of almond milk begins with a raw and unpasteurized nut. Almonds have a delicate floral sweetness that's only captured when the almond has not been processed. Almonds are one of the only system-alkalizing nuts, and they work miracles on the nervous system, skin, bones, and heart. Fresh almond milk floods the body with minerals, protein, omega-3 fatty acids, calcium, and antioxidants. It is also incredibly versatile in the kitchen, pairing well with virtually anything, and delicious to drink on its own. Almond pulp has endless applications, too, and is used in many of our sweet and savory preparations.

WALNUT MILK

Walnuts are one of the most nutrient-dense brain foods, providing high doses of alpha-linoleic and omega-3 fatty acids, antioxidants, minerals, and phytonutrients. Omega-3s are incredible for health and may prevent a wide range of physical ailments, including depression. These distinctively meaty and delicious brain-shaped nuggets also help to boost serotonin and dopamine, and provide critical cellular support.

Although I'm usually a purist, this milk seems to demand honey and cinnamon, as their flavors flatter the inherent beauty of the walnut.

HAZELNUT MILK

Hazelnut milk is a little luxury. It's on the less acidic side and lovely to have on hand for an impromptu pot of chocolate milk, pancake batters, or a warm nightcap with a touch of honey. Deeply mineralizing, alkalizing, and supportive of brain development, this potent milk also helps to regulate mood.

BRAZIL NUT MILK

A raw, truly fresh Brazil nut is very different from those you may have tasted from a can of mixed nuts. Brazil nuts are flush with essential fatty acids and trace minerals like selenium, which helps to regulate thyroid and immune function. They are among the most mineral-dense foods on earth, and are primarily still wild-harvested from the Amazon. They make for a hearty, almost meaty, and elegant milk that is very fortifying.

PUMPKIN SEED MILK

I fell in love with pumpkin seeds after going through a bottle of dark, thick pumpkin seed oil from a friend's family farm. The raw pressed pumpkin seed oil was so vibrant, and instead of its suggested pairing with bread, I used it as a dip for apples and endive leaves. I have not been able to find a commercial pumpkin seed oil of similar potency, but I enjoy the power of pumpkin seeds almost daily through unexpectedly delicate activated pumpkin seed milk.

The seeds, rich with minerals and fatty acids, not only satiate cravings for plant power, but they feed your brain and nervous system as well. In addition, pumpkin seeds balance the endocrine system, encouraging healthy hormone production. I especially enjoy making pumpkin seed milk in the fall and winter, as it goes well with persimmons, chocolate, squash, and roots.

HEMP AND COCONUT MILK

This unsoaked Minute Milk is the perfect combination of hemp seeds, coconut meat, vanilla bean, and pink salt. Hemp can have a very pronounced flavor that is not to everyone's liking, but mellowed by coconut and vanilla, it's a surprisingly neutral base for sweet milks. It's my go-to for a morning wake and shake. One of the greatest sources of plant protein and fat, hemp seeds boost the immune system, tame inflammation, help us burn fat and flush toxins, and nourish beauty. They are very alkalizing and high in amino acids and enzymes. Both coconut and hemp

support skin and the thyroid, while their plant proteins and fats serve as brain and muscle builders.

LAIT DE COCO

This ode to the creamy splendor of the coconut is a perfect staple milk. It goes from sweet to savory seamlessly, as good in a sweet Moon Milk as in a carrot ginger soup or a curry with squash and cilantro. I use two forms of coconut for a well-balanced coco vibe: The dried coconut provides a deep and meaty flavor, while the Thai coconut meat offers a sublime creamy texture and whip.

Coconut supports the thyroid, boosts the metabolism and immune system, helps to eliminate toxins, and is antifungal. Lait de Coco aids in balancing blood sugar and alleviates adrenal stress, making it the ideal milk to sip throughout the day. This is a great milk for anyone who is treating candida or a parasite, as it's a very powerful cleansing agent and is a good candidate for sweetening with a drop of stevia, as its high fat content really rounds out the flavor.

This milk supports the nervous system, skin, and hormone production. If you start to use this as your staple milk, you may feel a significant difference in your hair and skin. Best of all, because no soaking is needed, you're set up for a week of Lait de Coco with an investment of only one minute!

SESAME BUTTER MILK

When I was four, the Ayurvedic doctor who changed the course of my life told me to eat as many sesame seeds as I could. I took his advice to heart, and thirty years later what began as eating dried old seeds by the spoonful has been replaced by glasses of this rich milk.

This Minute Milk provides dense doses of iron to energize and fuel the body. High in iron, B vitamins, calcium, minerals, and proteins, sesame seeds are a great option for those who can't eat nuts, as they are a bioavailable, potent, and easily assimilated plant-based protein.

Using raw silky sesame butter instead of seeds produces a less bitter milk. (My hunch is that the butter may better preserve the sesame oils.) For a change you can even make a black-label version of the milk by using black sesame seeds. Made without honey, the milk is absolutely delicious blended with white miso and a little garlic and served warm.

WELL MILK CHART

ALL MAKE 4 CUPS (32 OUNCES)

	BENEFITS	INGREDIENTS	PREP	METHOD	BY-PRODUCTS
ALMOND MILK	Alkalizer Mineralizes deeply Plant protein	1 cup raw almonds 4½ cups water 2 pinches of pink salt 2 teaspoons raw honey, or to taste	Put the dry, raw almonds in a bowl and add enough water to cover. Soak in the fridge overnight.	Drain the nuts and transfer to a blender. Add the water and salt and blend on high for 30 to 45 seconds until the nuts are broken down and the liquid is milky. Don't overblend.	This pulp will be the basis of your most versatile pastry doughs and flours, including the Vanilla Pastry Dough (page 206) and Almond Pastry Dough (page 200).
WALNUT MILK	Brain activator Joy promoter Hormone balancer	1½ cups raw walnuts 4 cups water 2 pinches of pink salt 2 teaspoons raw honey ¼ teaspoon ground cinnamon	Put the dry, raw walnuts in a bowl and add enough water to cover. Soak in the fridge overnight.	Drain the walnuts and transfer to a blender. Add the water, salt, honey, and cinnamon. Blend on high until the nuts are broken down to a pulp and the liquid is milky, about 45 seconds.	Dehydrate the pulp and use in brownies, granola, and streusel.
BRAZIL NUT MILK	Beauty food Brain activator Energy food	1 cup raw Brazil nuts 4 cups water ⅛ teaspoon pink salt	Put the dry, raw Brazil nuts in a bowl and add enough water to cover. Soak in the fridge overnight.	Drain the nuts and transfer to a blender. Add the water and salt and blend on high until the nuts are broken down to a pulp and the liquid is milky, about 45 seconds.	Dehydrate the pulp and use in any of my pastry recipes; it's lighter in color and makes for pretty baked goods. The flour also adds a distinctive flavor to pancakes that is great with maple syrup.
HAZELNUT MILK	Alkalizer Beauty food Brain activator	1 cup raw hazelnuts 4 cups water Generous pinch of pink salt	Put the dry, raw hazelnuts in a bowl and add enough water to cover. Soak in the fridge overnight.	Drain the nuts and transfer to a blender. Add the water and salt and blend on high until the nuts are broken down to a pulp and the liquid is milky, about 45 seconds.	I love hazelnut pulp as much as the milk and will often go straight into hazelnut brownie mode rather than dehydrate it.

	BENEFITS	INGREDIENTS	PREP	METHOD	BY-PRODUCTS
PUMPKIN SEED MILK	Hormone balancer Mineralizes deeply Brain activator	1 cup raw pumpkin seeds 4 cups water 1½ teaspoons raw honey ¼ teaspoon pink salt	Put the dry, raw pumpkin seeds in a bowl and add enough water to cover. Soak in the fridge overnight.	Drain the seeds and transfer to a blender. Add the water, honey, and salt and blend until smooth. Pour the mixture into a fine-mesh sieve or nut bag and strain to remove the solids.	Pumpkin seed pulp would be excellent for breads, pancakes, and pound cakes paired with persimmon and other fall flavors.
LAIT DE COCO	Hormone balancer Metabolism booster Brain activator	⅓ cup unsweetened shredded coconut ¼ cup young Thai coconut meat (one 5 x 2-inch strip), fresh or frozen 4 cups water Pinch of pink salt	n/a	Combine all the ingredients in a blender and blend until smooth, about 45 seconds This milk will have a nice "cream on top" when cold, so shake and stir to evenly distribute.	Refrigerate the pulp for up to a week, or dehydrate and sneak the pulp into chocolate recipes or cookie dough for a hit of fiber.
HEMP AND COCONUT MILK	Brain activator Metabolism booster Hormone balancer	3 heaping tablespoons hemp seeds 4 teaspoons fresh or frozen young coconut 4 cups water Generous pinch of pink salt	n/a	Combine all the ingredients in a blender and blend on high for 45 seconds or until smooth. If you don't have a high-speed blender, proceed as above, blending for an extra 45 seconds, then strain through a nut milk bag. Milk made in a high-speed blender will not require straining.	n/a
SESAME BUTTER MILK	Energy food Mineralizes deeply Beauty food	2 tablespoons raw smooth sesame seed butter 4 cups water 2 teaspoons raw honey Generous pinch pink salt	n/a	Combine all the ingredients in a blender and blend on high until completely smooth, about 45 seconds.	n/a

CHAPTER 5

MOON MILKS, SHAKES & LATTES

Of all the recipes in this book, I may love the Moon Lattes best of all. Playing with blends of warm nut milks spiked with adaptogens and herbs was the thing that took my health journey to the next level. My life literally exploded after incorporating these potions into my daily routine. In the early days of Moon Juice, I relied on Deep Chocolate's synergistic blend of maca and cacao to keep me going.

Lattes are made with hot water, warm nut milk, or a combination of the two. Add a teaspoon of ghee or coconut oil along with your herbs of choice for a metabolism-boosting, brain-nourishing, hormone-balancing, satiating dose of good fat. Blend the ingredients in a high-speed blender; in less than a minute you should have a nice frothy cappuccino-like tonic. You can also make a double batch and enjoy some warm, then stash the rest in the fridge for the afternoon and shake with ice in a glass jar to make an iced latte.

Once you're comfortable making the Moon Milks, shakes, and lattes in this chapter, experiment with your own custom formulas, blending in the specific medicinal elements, organic spices, high-functioning foods, and low-glycemic sweeteners you need most to refine and power the body and mind.

MACA AND CACAO are right up there with caffeine and alcohol in their ability to alter mood and energy. Maca is an adaptogen, and cacao is my favorite high-functioning food—together they make a delicious malty chocolate shake that will have you feeling on top of the world. Add to this the brain-feeding powers of walnut milk, and you'll be capable of anything.

In fact, Deep Chocolate is the drink I get the most texts about from people reporting that it's taken them out of depression, saved their marriage by reviving their intimacy, and, of course, given them so much energy they're afraid something's wrong.

And unlike other substances that provide this kind of high, Deep Chocolate doesn't deplete you. You're only building a stronger and sexier endocrine system that can handle more and more efficiency, activity, and joy each day. A Deep Chocolate supercharged with whatever is calling to me from the pantry is a daily affair. I could go heavy on cordyceps if I'm feeling adrenally fatigued. I'll include a hit of cistanche for a powerful aphrodisiac, or chaga for immunity, or ashwagandha for stress relief. For a zero-glycemic version, use 2 drops liquid stevia in place of the honey.

DEEP CHOCOLATE MOON MILK

MAKES 16 OUNCES

JOY
PROMOTER

MINERALIZES
DEEPLY

ENERGY
FOOD

16 ounces Walnut Milk (page 100)
1½ teaspoons raw honey or
    sweetener of choice
2 tablespoons cacao powder
2 tablespoons maca powder
¼ teaspoon ground cinnamon
3 ice cubes

Combine all the ingredients in a blender and blend until smooth.

MOON DUSTING
My supercharged version of this is called the Deep Adaptogenic, and it includes a pea-size amount of shilajit, 1 teaspoon cordyceps, ¼ teaspoon reishi, and ⅛ teaspoon cayenne.

THIS SHAKE WAS inspired by the famous California date shakes that I have long been intrigued by but never able to enjoy because of my aversion to white sugar and pasteurized cow's milk. Each trip to Palm Desert inspired me to create a version that I could truly savor.

While traveling in Lebanon, I got into the habit of having an afternoon espresso with ground cardamom, which was always served with a single date. The combination of those flavors is the epitome of romance to me.

As I began working to boost my endocrine system, I started to incorporate a teaspoon of maca into my daily diet. I realized maca's nuttiness would perfectly pair with cardamom, coffee, dates, and creamy Brazil nut milk.

This drink represents the best of California kitsch and the romance of the Middle East—all wrapped up in an endocrine remedy.

DATE SHAKE

MAKES 16 OUNCES

ENERGY FOOD

APHRODISIAC

PLANT PROTEIN

16 ounces Brazil Nut Milk
  (page 100)
2 tablespoons maca powder
8 coffee beans
4 Medjool dates, pitted
2 pinches of ground cardamom

Pantry tip: Pit large bags of dates and pulse them in the food processor to turn them into a date paste (1 tablespoon date paste equals 1 date).

Combine all the ingredients in a blender and blend until thoroughly incorporated.

MOON DUSTING

I like to include ½ teaspoon ashwagandha, which offsets the tax the espresso bean could exert on your endocrine system and enhances thyroid support. I will also often add ½ teaspoon mucuna to this blend for an additional mood and libido boost. A tablespoon of tocotrienols will add to the decadence, as well as the beautifying skin food benefits of the Brazil nuts.

I STARTED USING TRUE COLLOIDAL SILVER to help heal wounds on my skin. It was an external remedy I'd long been familiar with, a potent antibiotic and antiviral concentration of the element. But I learned that when taken as a supplement, it boosts immunity.

Because I was used to taking strong-tasting immune aids, the day I found out colloidal silver had no taste, I began to sprinkle it everywhere. Colloidal silver is completely safe with normal use. As outlined by the Silver Safety Council, six drops daily is a harmless way to support your body inside and out.

As a mom, I'm always looking to multitask with food. If it's something that's tasty and is going to be consumed often, it should have a superpower. I chose a strawberry Moon Milk as a host for this medicine because I knew that everyone would love it, including children.

SILVER STRAWBERRY

MAKES 16 OUNCES

IMMUNITY
FOOD

PLANT
PROTEIN

ALKALIZER

2 cups Almond Milk (page 100)
¾ cup fresh or frozen
    strawberries
2 teaspoons raw honey, or 2 drops
    of stevia, or other sweetener of
    choice
6 drops colloidal silver

Combine all the ingredients in a blender and blend until thoroughly incorporated.

MOON DUSTING
A teaspoon of chaga doesn't alter the delicate strawberry freshness, and synergizes beautifully with the silver's immunity-boosting and cell-restoring powers.

I **CREATED THE CREAMY,** delicious Spiced Yam Moon Juice for women experiencing the symptoms of PMS and menopause, and it quickly became a cult hit. Yam is a powerful hormone balancer that can relieve related symptoms while radically improving short-term memory.

But I wanted to take both the medicinal qualities and the delicious mouthfeel of Spiced Yam even further. I added maca for hormone support and energy, lucuma as skin and brain food, and pumpkin seed milk to continue endocrine harmony. These additions transform this highly effective blend into a rich treat. This is really great served warm.

YAM JULIUS

THYROID SUPPORT

APHRODISIAC

HORMONE BALANCER

MAKES 16 OUNCES

1 cup Spiced Yam (page 86)
1 cup Pumpkin Seed Milk
    (page 101)
1 teaspoon lucuma powder
1 teaspoon maca powder

Combine all the ingredients in a blender and blend until thoroughly incorporated.

MOON DUSTING
Adding a teaspoon of ho shou wu will synergize the blend into the ultimate hormone tonic.

GOLDEN MILK IS THE CULT MOON MILK.

Years ago, unaware of its Ayurvedic roots, I naively conjured the idea of an ancient yogic recipe that added turmeric juice and spice into milk. This is a blend that really wants to be on the planet: From its resurrection in the Moon Juice kitchen to now being widely enjoyed by the masses, it is a luminous recipe that is equally healing and pleasurable.

Turmeric root has a thousand and one virtues, including inflammation-soothing properties that are as effective as a painkiller for me. I find it works within about twenty minutes to address joint pain.

This nourishing Moon Milk delivers lifetimes of pleasure and a multidimensional taste experience. It speaks to the magic of medicinal traditions that expand beyond time and space, recalling the ancient phenomena of Ayurveda. If you can't get fresh turmeric, you can substitute ½ teaspoon of ground turmeric but it will have a distinctly different flavor.

GOLDEN MILK

MAKES 16 OUNCES

INFLAMMATION TAMER

BEAUTY FOOD

DETOXIFIER

12 ounces Almond Milk (page 100)
¾ pound fresh turmeric, juiced
2 teaspoons raw honey or
    sweetener of choice
⅛ teaspoon ground cardamom
¼ teaspoon ground cinnamon
5 whole black peppercorns, or
    3 drops of black pepper oil

Combine all the ingredients in a blender and blend on high until the peppercorns have fully broken down.

MOON DUSTING
Enriching this golden potion with 1 teaspoon lucuma powder adds to the inflammation-taming benefits of the turmeric, and will help you cut down on the honey content, enhancing the inherent sweetness of the fresh turmeric root juice. Try halving your honey, or use none at all!

BEE POLLEN'S multihued golden granules charm me to no end as the product of a mystical dance between flowers and bees that can be held in your hands. This powerful alkaline food contains twenty-two amino acids and is heavy in bioavailable proteins and B vitamins. It's a beauty and muscle food, aphrodisiac, and thyroid supporter. I recommend finding a local beekeeper and getting pollen directly from them. If you can't purchase directly from a beekeeper, be sure to source truly raw bee pollen.

This combination of hemp milk and raw vanilla offers protein-rich post-workout fuel made from ingredients you likely have in your kitchen.

BEE POLLEN

THYROID
SUPPORT

PLANT
PROTEIN

APHRODISIAC

MAKES 16 OUNCES

1 tablespoon bee pollen, plus
   1 teaspoon for garnish
⅛ teaspoon raw vanilla bean
   powder
2 tablespoons coconut butter
16 ounces Hemp Milk (page 101)
½ teaspoon raw honey or
   sweetener of choice (optional,
   depending on inherent
   sweetness of your bee pollen)

Combine 1 tablespoon of the bee pollen, the vanilla powder, coconut butter, hemp milk, and sweetener (if using) in a blender. Blend until smooth. Pour into a glass and garnish with the remaining 1 teaspoon bee pollen.

MOON DUSTING
Adding a tablespoon of maca to this blend will bonify the energy-boosting, happy, sexy, fertility making to the max!

DRIED TURKISH FIGS are quite possibly one of my favorite things on the planet. One of the bestsellers at Moon Juice since we opened, Vanilla Fig highlights fig's jammy, musky flavor, which is accentuated by the addition of raw vanilla. It's combined with mineral-rich hazelnuts and lucuma.

VANILLA FIG

ALKALIZER

MINERALIZES DEEPLY

BEAUTY FOOD

MAKES 16 OUNCES

16 ounces Hazelnut Milk
    (page 100)
4 or 5 dried Turkish figs
2 teaspoons lucuma powder
1/8 teaspoon raw vanilla bean
    powder
1 teaspoon raw honey or
    sweetener of choice
3 ice cubes

Combine all the ingredients in a blender and blend thoroughly to break down the figs. The ice cubes will offset the heat generated by the longer blending, as the figs take some time to break down.

MOON DUSTING

Add a teaspoon of probiotics to work alongside the cleansing fig seeds for gut health and glowing skin. Adding 1/2 teaspoon pearl powder turns this into a real adaptogenic beauty milk, deeply mineralizing and fortifying cells from the inside out with aminos and antioxidants.

THIS MOON MILK IS ALCHEMIZED from a raw, activated, silky sesame butter that boosts the system with iron and B vitamins. Doses of tissue-regenerating lucuma support the skin and brain. Rich, green matcha blended with sesame, ginger, and lucuma creates a bright and nourishing milky potion.

Matcha is an incredibly energizing source of antioxidants that is gentle on the adrenals and boosts the metabolism. Instead of taxing the body, matcha provides a nourishing energy that supports the endocrine and nervous systems.

SESAME GINGER MATCHA

MAKES 16 OUNCES

16 ounces Sesame Butter Milk
    (page 101)
4 teaspoons fresh ginger juice
1 teaspoon raw honey or
    sweetener of choice
½ teaspoon matcha powder
½ teaspoon raw vanilla bean
    powder

Combine all the ingredients in a blender and blend until smooth. Serve cold or warmed.

MOON DUSTING

I love boosting the creaminess and vitamin content of the sesame milk with a tablespoon of detoxifying tocotrienols and their bioavailable vitamin E. A teaspoon of antiaging, antioxidant-rich lucuma pairs perfectly with the mineral-dense, antiaging properties of matcha.

ENERGY FOOD

IMMUNITY FOOD

DETOXIFIER

A BRILLIANT BLUE MIXTURE of Lait de Coco, Blue Majik E3Live, maca, mesquite, mint extract, and cacao nibs, this is a profoundly cooling, energizing, and refreshing bioavailable treat. A greens mix or spirulina work well in this blend if you don't have Blue Algae on hand. Our original recipe called for an ormus greens mix, but once I found this magic blue source, I became a convert.

BLUE MINT CHIP

MAKES 16 OUNCES

16 ounces Lait de Coco (page 101)
2 teaspoons raw honey or
    sweetener of choice
1 tablespoon maca powder
1 tablespoon mesquite powder
½ teaspoon pure peppermint
    extract
¼ teaspoon blue algae
1 tablespoon cacao nibs

Combine the Lait de Coco, honey, maca, mesquite powder, peppermint extract, and blue algae in a blender and blend until well combined. Add the cacao nibs and blend for 10 to 12 seconds—you don't want to overblend your chips!

MOON DUSTING
I love adding 1 teaspoon mucuna for the brain-stimulating benefits, alongside the algae, maca, and cacao. You can also substitute blue-green algae for the blue algae for a similar flavor, different color.

HORMONE
BALANCER

ENERGY
FOOD

JOY
PROMOTER

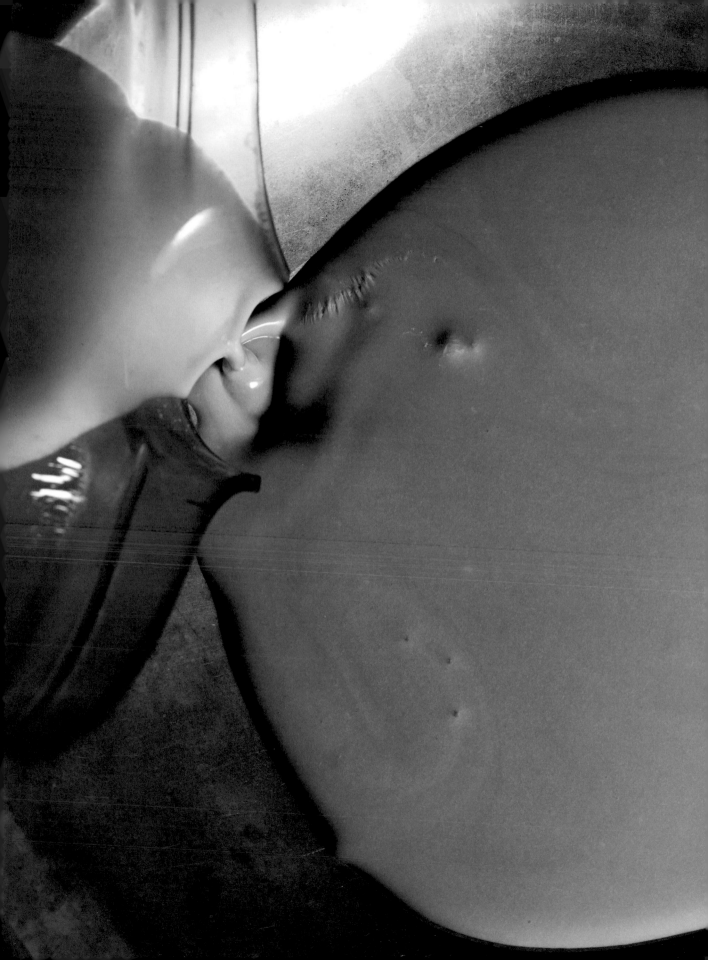

I AM ALWAYS LOOKING for new ways to make completely sugar-free treats that don't involve frozen bananas—I love the texture the fruit provides, but their sugar is a bit much for my system. As a zero-glycemic alternative, I started freezing avocados and keeping them on hand for hot summer days when I am craving a thick, frosty milk shake.

Frozen avocado is a dreamy, creamy way to get the perfect shake texture without any of the sugar. If I'm on a roll, I may use half an avocado a day, and I like to freeze a month's worth at once. Just peel, pit, and quarter the avocados and place in the freezer on a baking sheet until frozen solid. You can then transfer the quarters to a resealable plastic bag. Squeeze out as much air as possible, seal, and keep frozen until ready to use.

This malt is a thick, supremely decadent chocolate shake that puts any soda fountain fantasies of mine to shame. It's everything decadent about a shake with zero sugar, a good dose of raw, healthy fat, and supercharged energy from cacao and activated walnuts. If you don't want to use stevia, use a sweetened Well Milk.

ZERO-GLYCEMIC FROSTY CHOCOLATE MALT

MAKES 12 OUNCES

BRAIN ACTIVATOR

ENERGY FOOD

MINERALIZES DEEPLY

8 ounces Deep Chocolate Moon Milk (page 104), made without sweetener
¼ avocado, pitted, peeled, and frozen for at least 4 hours
⅛ teaspoon raw vanilla bean powder
¼ cup ice cubes
3 or 4 drops of stevia

Combine all the ingredients in a blender and blend on high until smooth. Don't overblend your frosty drink, as it will cause the ice to melt.

LET ME HIT YOU with my green juice and avocado sales pitch—yet again! This is a great way to energize yourself throughout the day, offering energy from the green juice, beautifying and brain power from the avocado, adaptogenic energy and libido boost from maca, and it can all be zero glycemic if you choose to use stevia.

It's thick and frozen. Depending on how thick you want it to be, you can add more frozen avocado. It could even turn into a green ice cream or a green shake bowl topped with bee pollen, hemp seeds, cacao chips, chopped nuts, or anything else that will make you happy.

For my son, Rohan, I add ½ teaspoon mint extract and garnish with cacao nibs for an amazing mint chip ice cream version.

THE GREEN SHAKE

MAKES 12 OUNCES

ENERGY
FOOD

JOY
PROMOTER

DETOXIFIER

10 ounces Goodness Greens
(page 70)
¼ cup water
½ avocado, pitted, peeled, and
frozen for at least 4 hours
1 tablespoon maca powder
1 tablespoon almond butter
2 drops of stevia or other
sweetener of choice

Combine the ingredients in a blender and blend on high just until smooth. Don't overblend or you will begin to heat your frosty drink. Pour into a glass and serve with a garnish if you like.

MOON DUSTINGS
My power blend includes cordyceps, for stamina and adrenal support. A skin food version includes 1 tablespoon tocotrienols and 1 tablespoon lucuma.

A LUSTY ADAPTOGENIC BREW to ignite and excite sexy flow in both men and women, this warming elixir sends power to all the right places while also supporting your primal life-force. It's an edible holistic addition to your sexual and creative play. I like to make it with pumpkin seeds because they are rich in zinc, which is not only good for the skin and brain but also supports the prostate, and the pumpkin flavor pairs beautifully with the chocolate, cinnamon, and cayenne. That said, use any Well Milk you like best. The addition of coconut oil or ghee will do wonders for sustained energy.

HOT SEX MILK

MAKES 12 OUNCES

APHRODISIAC

ENERGY FOOD

JOY PROMOTER

12 ounces Pumpkin Seed Milk
   (page 101)
1 tablespoon maca powder
1 tablespoon cacao powder
1 teaspoon ho shou wu
1 teaspoon ghee or coconut oil
¼ teaspoon ground schisandra
   berries
⅛ teaspoon cayenne
1 teaspoon bee pollen, for garnish

Gently warm the pumpkin seed milk (it should be just warm, not hot) in a small saucepan and carefully pour it into a blender. Add the maca, cacao, ho shou wu, ghee, schisandra berries, and cayenne. Blend on high for 20 seconds or until warm and frothy. Pour into a mug and serve garnished with the bee pollen.

THE ESSENCES OF HIBISCUS AND ROSE combine with goji and schisandra berries to create a cooling, tonifying, hydrating sipping tonic that is deeply beautifying. Hibiscus and rose both quench heat in the body, which can manifest as redness, rashes, or acne. Hibiscus is also a powerful flush to the system, helping to gently cleanse the kidneys, doing a wonderful and immediate job at reducing any puffiness in your face. Schisandra and goji berries are the crown jewels of traditional Chinese beauty secrets. While the schisandra hydrates from the inside out for healthy, supple skin at any age, the nutrient-dense goji berries team up to deeply nourish and increase elastin and collagen. The drink is also very high in vitamin C, great for healing as well as skin health. Make a big jug to keep in your fridge and enjoy it hot or cold. You can also make a more concentrated version by using half as much water. Use it to spike sparkling water, lovely for entertaining.

PETAL AND BERRY BEAUTY TONIC

BEAUTY
FOOD

APHRODISIAC

STRESS
RELIEVER

MAKES 32 OUNCES

4 cups water
½ cup goji berries
¼ cup dried hibiscus flowers
1 teaspoon ground schisandra
   berries
2 teaspoons rose water
Raw honey or stevia (optional)

Bring the water to a boil. Place the goji berries, hibiscus, and schisandra in a 1-quart glass jar.

Add enough boiling water to cover and set aside to steep for 1 hour. Strain, reserving the solids for a second batch if you like (I also like to snack on the plumped goji berries, or you can blend them into a smoothie, coconut yoghurt, or nut milk for a vibrant sunset color). Stir in the rose water and sweetener (if using). Enjoy immediately or cover and store in the fridge for up to a week to enjoy hot, chilled, or combined with sparkling water.

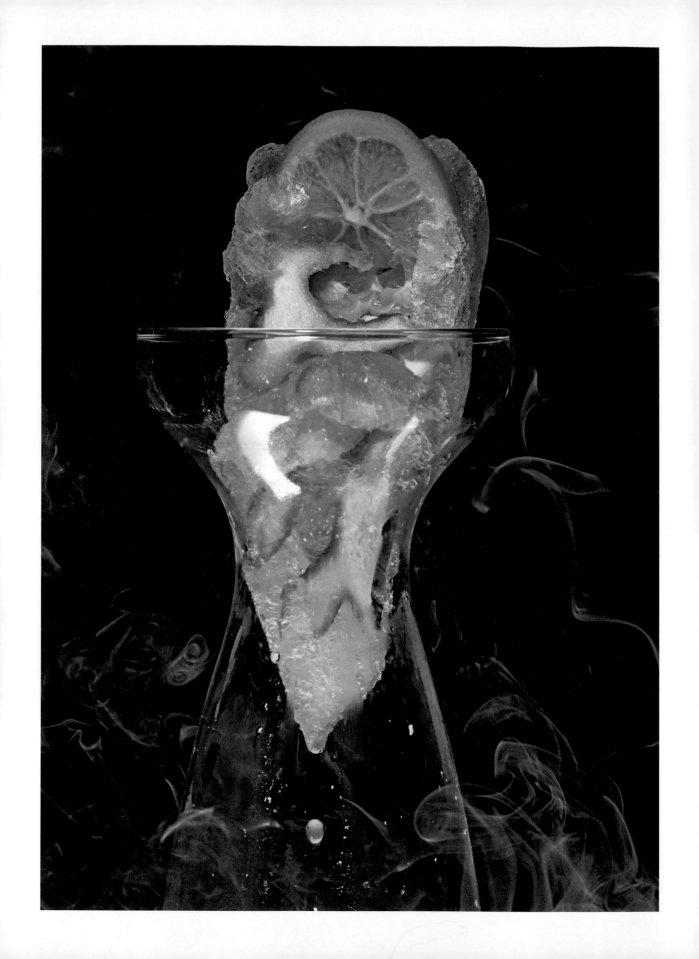

SOCIALIZING AROUND A FIRE with a hot beverage is among my favorite autumnal activities. Warm apple cider is always a bit too sweet for me, though, and I miss the medicinally potent zing I get from a boozy hot toddy. This recipe captures both the potency and essence of a toddy while delivering true benefits.

MOON TODDY

SERVES 4

IMMUNITY
FOOD

DIGESTIVE
AID

DETOXIFIER

32 ounces Gingered Lemon
　　(page 81)
2 tablespoons apple cider vinegar
1 tablespoon colloidal silver
4 pinches of cayenne, for garnish

Gently warm the Gingered Lemon in a saucepan over low heat, without allowing it to simmer. Remove from the heat and add the vinegar and silver. Divide the toddy among four mugs and float a pinch of cayenne on each serving.

A CARAMEL-Y LATTE, alchemized to energize the spirit, relieve stress, and impart feelings of centeredness and strength, this is a delightful adaptogenic system regulator. The reishi and mucuna deftly elevate mood, inspire creativity, regulate sleep patterns, and even ignite libido while soothing the nerves and inflammation, and boosting immunity and liver function. Sip it morning, noon, or midnight. The adaptogenic qualities lend themselves to be energizing or calming, depending on what your system needs and the time of day.

BLISS BRAIN

MAKES 12 OUNCES

JOY PROMOTER

BRAIN ACTIVATOR

STRESS RELIEVER

12 ounces Walnut Milk (page 100)
1 tablespoon mesquite powder
½ teaspoon mucuna powder
½ teaspoon ashwagandha
½ teaspoon reishi powder
½ teaspoon raw vanilla bean powder
1 teaspoon ghee or coconut oil
Sweetener (I use 1 teaspoon raw honey or coconut sap, or 1 drop of stevia for a low-glycemic version)

Gently warm the walnut milk in a saucepan over low heat, without allowing it to simmer. Carefully pour it into a blender. Add the mesquite powder, mucuna, ashwagandha, reishi, vanilla, oil, and sweetener. Blend on high for 20 seconds or until warm and frothy. Pour into a mug and enjoy.

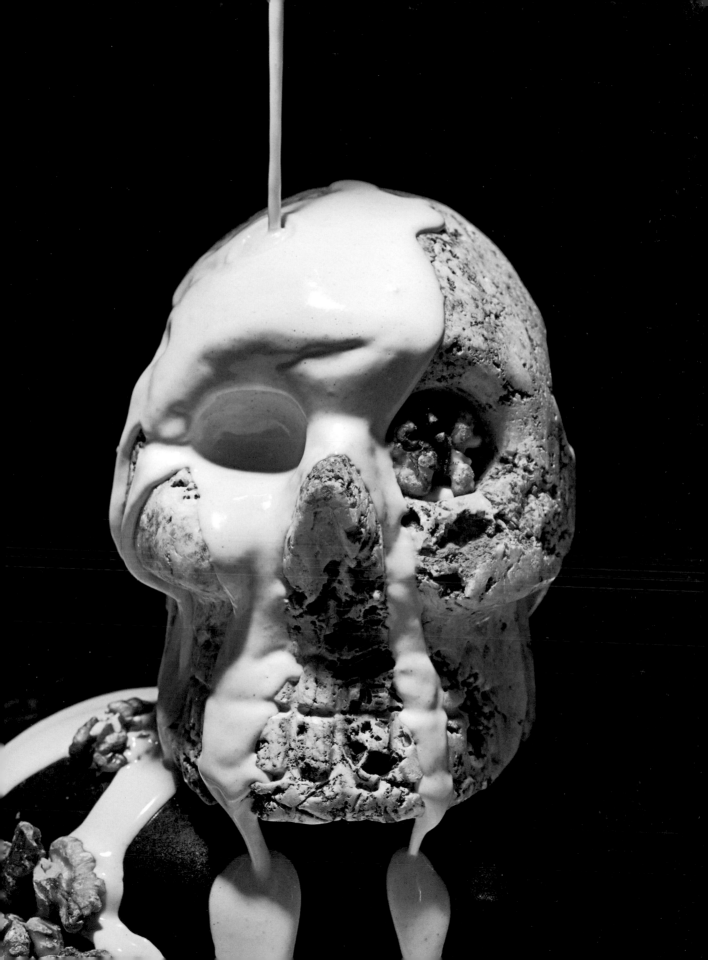

THIS IS A WARM CUP of luscious antioxidant, enzyme, amino, and mineral richness. This ancient beauty potion delivers deep nourishment into the bloodstream for bone and cell building and tissue regeneration, reversing the effects of aging and inflammation. It also tonifies and heals organs, beautifying on a cellular level and bringing suppleness to the skin and shine to hair.

BEAUTY LATTE

MAKES 12 OUNCES

12 ounces Lait de Coco (page 101)
1 teaspoon rose water
2 teaspoons lucuma powder
¼ teaspoon pearl powder
½ teaspoon ground schisandra berries
1 teaspoon raw honey or coconut sap, or 1 drop of stevia for a low-glycemic version
1 teaspoon ghee or coconut oil
1 tablespoon tocotrienols

Gently warm the Lait de Coco in a saucepan over low heat, without allowing it to simmer. Carefully pour it into a blender. Add the rose water, lucuma, pearl, schisandra, sweetener, and oil. Blend on high for 20 seconds or until warm and frothy. Pour into a mug and serve topped with the tocotrienols.

BEAUTY FOOD

JOY PROMOTER

STRESS RELIEVER

THIS IS THE HOLISTIC, sustainable, energizing ritual to add to your life. After lots of tinkering and tweaking, I've locked into this blend, a high-functioning, brain-activating, mineralizing, metabolism-boosting potion that contains more than eighteen amino acids. At the same time, it's the adaptogenic endocrine champion, stress manager, and stamina longevity elevator. It was a game changer for my energy levels, and there are days that call for three cups of the stuff.

NOT COFFEE

MAKES 12 OUNCES

12 ounces Lait de Coco (page 101)
1 tablespoon maca powder
2 teaspoons cacao powder
1 teaspoon cordyceps powder
1 pea-size ball of shilajit resin, or
   1 teaspoon shilajit powder
¼ teaspoon ground cinnamon
Sweetener (I use 1½ teaspoons
   raw honey or coconut sap,
   or 2 drops of stevia for a
   zero-glycemic version)
1 teaspoon coconut oil or ghee

Gently warm the Lait de Coco in a saucepan over low heat, without allowing it to simmer. Carefully pour it into a blender. Add the maca, cacao, cordyceps, shilajit, cinnamon, sweetener, and oil. Blend on high for 20 seconds or until warm and frothy. Pour into a mug and thrive!

ENERGY
FOOD

BRAIN
ACTIVATOR

APHRODISIAC

THIS IS THE COZIEST, most warming, immunizing tonic to come home to, an intoxicating, nourishing antioxidant- and mineral-rich chocolate mugful topped with a creamy cloud of bioavailable vitamin E to support the lungs and tame inflammation. It incorporates two of the most powerful immortality mushrooms on earth, making it a cell-protecting immunizer to fuel recovery and longevity.

IMMUNITY HOT CHOCOLATE

MAKES 12 OUNCES

12 ounces Sesame Butter Milk (page 101), warmed
1½ tablespoons cacao powder
1 teaspoon chaga powder
½ teaspoon reishi powder
⅛ teaspoon ground cinnamon
1 tablespoon ghee or coconut oil
Sweetener (I use 2 teaspoons raw honey or coconut sap, or 3 drops of stevia for a zero-glycemic version)
1 tablespoon tocotrienols

Gently warm the Sesame Butter Milk in a saucepan over low heat, without allowing it to simmer. Carefully pour it into a blender. Add the cacao, chaga, reishi, cinnamon, ghee, and sweetener. Blend on high for 20 seconds or until warm and frothy. Pour into a mug and top with the tocotrienols.

IMMUNITY
FOOD

BRAIN
ACTIVATOR

BEAUTY
FOOD

BROTH BOWLS

I think of broth bowls as a warm and juicy salad, or a grainless bowl. Gather all the components you would want to eat for lunch or dinner, then slice, dice, or shave them into a bowl and pour warm broth over them. These are especially welcome in the colder months when the idea of eating salads is not as appealing, but served chilled or at room temperature, they are beautifully refreshing and equally delicious in the summer. I also love to pour broth over spiralized zucchini, carrots, or kelp noodles for a noodle-ly veggie bowl. However you serve your broth bowl, a dollop of cultured vegetables to finish will provide additional texture, flavor, and a healthy dose of probiotics.

ANDALUSIAN GAZPACHO

Blend 2 cups cold Almond Milk with ½ cup white grapes, ½ cup chopped cucumber, ¼ cup olive oil, and 1 tablespoon cider vinegar.

SEA ZOODLE SOUP

Pour warm Sea Bone Broth over spiralized strands of zucchini or daikon. Top with cultured veggies.

HERBED MUSHROOM BOWL

Pour warm Sea Bone Broth over shaved mushrooms, pattypan squash, and thyme. Garnish with basil.

THE GREEN BOWL

Pour warm Lazy Green Broth over sliced avocado, julienned radishes, and cilantro sprigs. Add a dash of chili oil.

THIS IS MY VERSION OF BONE BROTH: I think of kombu as sea bones. This broth is deeply nourishing, mineralizing, thyroid supporting, and warming. It's also iodine rich.

Kombu broth is so easy it's almost thoughtless—all you have to do is throw the elements in the pot.

This broth is perfect on its own, but will inspire days of creations. You can elaborate upon it by adding a tablespoon of ghee and drinking it in a mug or adding cultured vegetables for a warm and chunky soup. You can use it as a base for any puree or soup you make in the blender, you can steam grains in it (I add it to my rice cooker with quinoa), or you can steam vegetables in it for a soup.

It's also a great addition to any juice feast you might partake in, over any number of days.

I make this either weekly or quarterly, storing large batches in the freezer to defrost as needed.

SEA BONE BROTH

MINERALIZES DEEPLY

THYROID SUPPORT

IMMUNITY FOOD

MAKES ABOUT 3 QUARTS

12 cups water
10 dried kombu strips
4 leeks, dark green ends trimmed, halved through the root, and cleaned
1 cup dried shiitake mushrooms
1 tablespoon grated fresh ginger
3 scallions, sliced on an angle

In a large pot, bring the water to a boil. Add the kombu, leeks, and mushrooms and reduce the heat to low. Cover and simmer for 1 hour. Strain the broth, reserving the kombu, leeks, and mushrooms. Return the broth to the pot. Slice the vegetables and return them to the broth to eat as soup, or leave the broth as is. Garnish with the ginger and scallions.

PARTICULARLY DURING THE COLDER MONTHS, keep your system warm using this broth. You can drink it for a winter breakfast, or sip on it in a mug all day long.

A favorite meal is a huge salad made of sprouts, microgreens, or chiffonade of a heartier chard or beet green tossed with olive oil and fermented green vegetables with hot broth poured over it. It's a bowl, broth, soup, and salad in one. You can expand and add any grain or protein, but give this one a try! It's surprisingly satisfying.

LAZY GREEN BROTH

PLANT
PROTEIN

ENERGY
FOOD

IMMUNITY
FOOD

MAKES ABOUT 1½ CUPS

1 cup hot water
1 tablespoon miso
1 tablespoon extra-virgin olive oil
1 teaspoon spirulina
1 garlic clove
Juice of 1 lemon
Pinch of cayenne

Combine all the ingredients in a blender and blend on high until the garlic has completely broken down, 20 to 40 seconds.

IF YOU HAVEN'T CAUGHT ON YET, I'll confess: I'm on a mission to get you to love sea vegetables and green juice more than you already do. This is one of my secret weapons. I have many fond memories of Spanish gazpacho, which I always think of with bright red tomatoes and toasted bread on a hot afternoon. I love the temperature of the soup, the cleansing kick from the sherry vinegar, and the garlic.

I took these elements out and added them to our healthy best friends of kelp, green juice, and avocado. The only joy missing is an afternoon in Barcelona.

This is a thyroid-nourishing, iodine-rich, bright, energizing, beautifying, and cleansing blend. I highly recommend this for entertaining, to start a meal, or as a passed appetizer in a shot glass or a small bowl. You can garnish the gazpacho with julienned kelp, a slice of avocado, and a drizzle of olive oil.

GREEN JUICE & KELP GAZPACHO

MAKES 2 CUPS

1 avocado
½ medium cucumber
12 ounces any unsweetened green juices
Handful of fresh cilantro leaves (about ½ cup)
½ jalapeño, seeded
¼ cup fresh or soaked kelp
Juice of ½ lime
½ clove garlic
Pink salt to taste

Combine all the ingredients except the salt in a blender and blend until smooth. Taste and add salt if needed; depending on how much you've soaked and rinsed the kelp, there may be enough salt left in it to go without additional salt.

CHAPTER 6

YOGHURT, KEFIR & CHEESE

This section is all about fermented creamy goodness. Fermentation is a method of preserving food that is an equally powerful method of preserving your health. I eat something fermented every day—and no, not sourdough or beer. Eating fermented foods is a great way to culture your gut, or digestive system, which is the true foundation of good health. Fermented foods are also exceptional sources of probiotics.

You can eat cultured foods multiple times a day, from kefir in the morning to cultured veggies with every meal to indulging in probiotic cream cheese icing. I even incorporate them into dehydrated crackers that I eat in the car on my daily commute. Making cultured and fermented foods does require planning and forethought, but as with most aspects of the Moon Kitchen, it will soon become a habitual and enjoyable part of your weekly kitchen practice.

WHAT IS A PROBIOTIC?

Probiotics are healthy bacteria that nurture intestinal microflora, heal the gut, and recolonize intestines with organisms that defend against disease, viruses, and yeast. Probiotics boost nutrient assimilation and decrease sugar cravings.

Foods high in probiotics will help deliver smoother digestion, stronger immunity, increased energy, elevated mood, glowing skin, and potent liver cleansing.

Let's take a moment to deal with the issue of bacteria head on. You are covered in bacteria, inside and out. Yet we've been told to disinfect and kill bacteria whenever possible. But being bacteria-free is not a healthy state of being; without any bacteria, you open yourself up to hosting whatever bacteria gets there first, and they may not necessarily be friendly.

So let's all appreciate and acknowledge that we live in a bacterial world. We can then start to call in the friendly bacteria that will curate our bacterial experience. Our world is alive with bacteria, and our bodies are filled with it. If we are going to be crawling with bacteria, let us find the ones we can have a healthy, symbiotic relationship with.

PROBIOTIC SUPPLEMENTS VERSUS CULTURED FOODS

The day I found out I could satiate my constant desire for creamy fermented dairy with coconut was a life-changing one. When I figured out how easy yoghurt and kefir were to make at home, they became one of my favorite ways to replace the lovely creaminess of dairy and increase my consumption of probiotics at the same time. Now I use probiotic supplements only in acute situations: for travel, at the onset or duration of illness, or if I've had three pizzas, for example. On a daily basis, these cultured and fermented foods are my primary source of probiotics, and when they become a part of your daily diet, you will have little need for additional supplementation.

The fat in the young Thai coconut meat that is the basis of the yoghurt, and is great for the immune system and thyroid, and is a wonderful beauty food. When inoculated with a powerful probiotic, coconut oil is very effective at killing bad bacteria. And while coconut water has relatively high sugar content, in the fermentation process, the bacteria will feed on the natural sugars, resulting in a less sweet final product.

You can find whole young Thai coconuts at the grocery store, and extract the meat by cracking them open with a cleaver or the back of a knife and scraping out the flesh with a spoon.

An easier option, however, is to buy the coconut already extracted from its shell. My favorite supplier is a certified organic company that shucks the coconut meat in Thailand, flash-freezes it, and ships it frozen. This coconut can be found at specialty health food shops and co-ops, or ordered online. Depending on how big your freezer is, you can stock up to have a constant flow of the ingredient for daily yoghurt.

Kefir, a cultured food similar to yoghurt but with a thinner, drinkable consistency, has been used throughout the ages. It is traditionally made with dairy and kefir grains that have traveled with humanity for centuries. I prefer a nondairy coconut version for these historically miraculous benefits, although kefir can be made from almond milk, too. Drink kefir just as is, or use it to create sodas. Adding kefir to your Moon Milks is also a way to incorporate the probiotic element into your day.

A note on probiotic starter: The yoghurt recipes in this book are made using our Moon Pantry probiotics, which are custom made in small batches to ensure potency. To make kefir, you can use the same probiotic I recommend for the yoghurt recipes or find your own kefir grains. These grains can be sourced from small, fringe communities online, but if you start talking about kefir and fermented foods with people, you may find friends and neighbors nearby who are already using kefir grains and cultures and are happy to share.

MOON POTS

Moon pots are really the pinnacle of fancy lazy. By using even a simple rocks glass, you can take elements like chia seeds soaked in milk or juice, coconut yoghurt, or avocado chocolate mousse, and bring in elements from your pantry like streusel, granola, Maca Mesquite Walnuts, or some of the raw nuts and seeds you will keep on hand.

Growing up as a New Yorker in the eighties, a "healthy treat" was a pasteurized cup of sweetened yoghurt with fruit on the bottom. It's been a winding road from there, but now I can have a blueberry yoghurt—or one with rose and pistachios, or cacao, or even savory ingredients—that I love even more and that is actually good for me. Much as I do with the Soft Cheese Base (see page 159), I try always to have an unflavored, unsweetened batch in my fridge as the jump-off to layering and dessert making.

Let your pots really reflect the season. In the summertime my pots are berry- and stone fruit–based, with chia and yoghurt to provide the fat and protein I need for the day while letting the fruit be the hero. In the winter, my pots might feature warmed overnight oats layered with bananas, persimmon, pears, and melted chocolate. By simply layering these foods that you will already have at your fingertips into a clear glass, you will have something beautiful to enjoy as breakfast, snack, or dessert.

These pots can also be warm and savory, and even graduate into bowls for a more substantial meal. My favorite bowls include a scoop of warmed savory chia, with a tangle of shaved or spiralized carrots that I'd tossed with some tomato jam. Another scoop of savory chia goes on top, with some cultured veggies or sea vegetables and a sprinkle of chopped dulse to finish. These would make a great passed app if you composed them in shot glasses. They also store really well, so if I'm entertaining, or even just want to set myself up with a bunch of grab-and-go snacks, I might build as many as ten at a time.

APRICOT, WALNUT & MULBERRY YOGHURT POT

Coconut Yoghurt, dried mulberries, chopped walnuts and apricots

SPICED YAM CHIA POT

use the same ratio as milk for Spiced Yam juice to chia (no need to sweeten), layer with Coconut Yoghurt and Maca Mesquite Walnuts

ROSE PISTACHIO YOGHURT POT

Coconut Yoghurt, fresh beet juice, stevia, rose water, dried rose petals, pistachios

CARROT PUDDING POT

enrich Coconut Yoghurt with a splash of carrot juice. Layer with Reishi Granola and garnish with black sesame seeds and a pinch of matcha powder.

PROBIOTIC HAZELNUT CRUNCH SUNDAE

Coconut Yoghurt, yacon syrup, Hazelnut Crunchers or cacao nibs

CHERRY CHOCOLATE CHIA POT

layer Cherry Black Pepper Jam, Chia Pudding with cacao whisked in, and Hazelnut Mesquite Streusel

BLUEBERRY LIME COCONUT YOGHURT POT

Coconut Yoghurt, crushed blueberries, a squeeze of lime juice, lime zest

ZUCCHINI NOODLE POT

layer Kitchari Chia Pudding, zucchini noodles tossed with lime juice, another scoop of the kitchari pudding, garnish with Turmeric, Coconut & Lime Pepitas

PLAIN COCONUT YOGHURT is a staple in my fridge and a great launching point for a huge diversity of composed yoghurts. It can be made in large batches that get tangier with time. I like my yoghurt taken to the breaking point of fermentation—there is a point at which the yoghurt will look completely curdled. This won't happen in your fridge, however.

This plain yoghurt base can be used for a variety of flavored savory and sweet yoghurts, smoothies, puddings, ice creams, cheesecakes, and frostings. Blend it with fruit to make ice pops, add it to raw cake batter, or serve it for dessert with fresh berries or cacao and maca.

On the savory front, you can thin it out with olive oil and use as a dip for crudités, add it to a soup, spread it as a base for avocado toast as you would mayonnaise, or flavor it with herbs as in the raita recipe on page 149. With so many diverse uses, you can see why I make this weekly. See page 154 to turn your coconut water into kefir.

COCONUT YOGHURT

MAKES 3 CUPS

PROBIOTIC

BEAUTY FOOD

IMMUNITY FOOD

12 ounces Thai coconut meat
   (2 cups)
1 cup water
½ teaspoon probiotics

Combine the coconut and water in a blender and puree until silky smooth. Transfer the mixture to a 1-quart glass jar and use a wooden spoon or a straw to stir in the probiotics. Cover the opening of the jar with a piece of cheesecloth or cotton.

Put it in the dehydrator on the lowest possible setting or set it on top of your stove with the oven on a very low heat; it should be just warm to the touch. You can place a folded kitchen towel underneath the glass container to protect your yoghurt from contact with heat that might be too intense, which will kill the probiotic microbes. Taste the yoghurt after 8 hours; you can tell it's ready when it becomes a bit fluffier and it tastes tangy.

DURING THE YEARS I SPENT WORKING in restaurants I developed very deep relationships with certain recipes that now feel like old friends. Raita, a traditional Indian seasoned yoghurt condiment, is one such old friend, as we spent a couple of seasons together at Lucques, a restaurant in Los Angeles.

It perfectly balances the sour notes of fermentation with the fat of yoghurt and olive oil and the accentuation of salt, letting the herbs and spices sing.

My favorite way to use this raita is to spoon it on roasted vegetables like kabocha squash or over a quinoa bowl, dollop it onto soup, or stir it into a chickpea curry.

SHALLOT & MINT RAITA

MAKES 2¾ CUPS

½ cup finely diced peeled and
    seeded cucumber
¼ cup finely diced shallot
2 teaspoons pink salt, plus more if
    needed
Juice of ½ lemon
2 cups Coconut Yoghurt (page 146)
3 tablespoons sliced fresh mint
    leaves
Freshly ground black pepper
¼ cup olive oil

In a medium bowl, combine the cucumber, shallot, salt, and lemon juice and set aside for 10 to 20 minutes. Drain off and discard any liquid that accumulates in the bowl, then add the yoghurt. Gently fold together and add more salt, if desired. Transfer to a serving dish or storage container. Serve garnished with the mint, pepper, and olive oil.

PROBIOTIC

BEAUTY
FOOD

JOY
PROMOTER

CHIA PUDDING was one of my first forays into playing with raw plant foods and experiencing real culinary joy from the simple process and its result. As a kid I loved the fish-eyes of tapioca pudding, so chia's shape and texture naturally appealed to me, and unlike starchy tapioca, chia is a perfect plant protein that rivals salmon in both protein and omega-3 content.

A successful chia pudding begins with a thorough, loving, constant stirring for a couple of minutes, much like a risotto. You can make chia with any of the Well Milks. My favorite is almond milk, though I'm also quite happy with chia seeds prepared in water with vanilla and a couple drops of stevia.

This chia pudding has the luxurious texture, flavor, and fragrance that can only be achieved with homemade almond milk. It's gently sweetened with coconut nectar, though you can also try honey or stevia. Feel free to add seasonal fruits, nuts, hemp seeds, cacao, and maca.

If you don't like the slightly gelatinous texture, you can pulse the chia in a blender. Chia pudding can be gently warmed on a winter's morning, more aggressively sweetened for a dessert, or made extra thick for a pie filling. It can also be added to any smoothie or Moon Milk recipe for extra substance.

CHIA PUDDING

ENERGY
FOOD

BRAIN
ACTIVATOR

MAKES 6 CUPS

⅓ cup coconut nectar
2 teaspoons raw vanilla bean
　powder
4 cups Almond Milk (page 100)
¾ cup chia seeds

In a small bowl, whisk together the nectar and vanilla with a small amount of the almond milk. In a medium bowl, whisk together the remaining milk, coconut nectar mixture, and the chia seeds. Whisk vigorously for 3 minutes. Refrigerate until the mixture has a puddinglike consistency, 30 to 45 minutes, whisking every 10 minutes. Enjoy immediately or cover and refrigerate for 3 to 5 days.

CHIA PUDDING has always been celebrated as a one-trick pony, but if you are avoiding grains, you can use a savory version just as you would a soft risotto or polenta. You can heat the pudding over a double boiler while still keeping it "raw," or if eating strictly raw is not a concern, you can simply heat it in a small saucepan over low heat, stirring often and being careful not to warm it to a boil, which will curdle and break the nut milk. Serve the warm savory pudding whenever you might have reached for quinoa or rice. Make Moon Pots or bowls, adding hot sauce, pickles, fresh herbs, shaved vegetables, and seaweed. You can puree a savory chia pudding in a blender to create a smooth dip that is not nut or legume based. Here I've combined an Indian spice blend known as kitchari, a blend of mustard, cumin, turmeric, and other warm spices, with coconut milk and carrot juice for a bright orange savory pudding. Serve it over zucchini noodles if you like.

KITCHARI CHIA PUDDING

MAKES 6 CUPS

1 tablespoon kitchari spice mix
1 teaspoon pink salt
3 cups Lait de Coco (page 101)
1 cup fresh carrot juice
¾ cup chia seeds

In a small bowl, whisk together the kitchari spice and salt with a small amount of the coconut milk. In a medium bowl, whisk together the remaining milk, carrot juice, and chia seeds. Stir in the seasoning mixture and whisk vigorously for 3 minutes. Refrigerate until the mixture has a puddinglike consistency, 30 to 45 minutes, whisking every 10 minutes. Enjoy immediately or cover and store in the refrigerator for 3 to 5 days.

BRAIN ACTIVATOR

DIGESTIVE AID

THIS IS ANOTHER FERMENTED coconut recipe to have on hand all the time. Coconut kefir is the ultimate hydrating, alkalizing, deeply mineralizing tonic. If you're getting fresh coconuts, making kefir goes hand in hand with yoghurt making. If you're going hard and making a month's worth of yoghurt out of fresh coconuts, you will be left with gallons of fresh coconut water that has a short shelf life and contains a lot of sugar.

My recommendation: Culture the coconut water to extend its shelf life and turn it into kefir for a profoundly immunizing, energizing, uplifting, and beautiful ferment. I drink a couple ounces of kefir first thing in the morning, or whenever I have a sugar craving.

I like to let my kefir go really far in its fermentation so it has a tight bubble. I also like to add stevia to mine, but you can stir in any type of sweetener you like or simply leave it unsweetened. You can even use coconut kefir as a "mother" with which to inoculate yoghurts and future batches of kefir and cultured veggies.

Sometimes, I'll whisk in 1 teaspoon of cacao powder for an egg crème variation, reminiscent of the soda fountain crèmes I used to drink with my dad while growing up in New York.

COCONUT KEFIR

MAKES 2 CUPS

DIGESTIVE AID

BEAUTY FOOD

IMMUNITY FOOD

2 cups raw coconut water
½ teaspoon probiotic

Pour the coconut water into a 1-quart glass jar and use a wooden spoon or straw to stir in the probiotics. Cover the opening of the jar with a piece of cheesecloth or cotton and secure it with a rubber band. Let the kefir stand at room temperature for 24 to 72 hours, depending on the temperature of your kitchen and the desired amount of "sparkle."

THIS ALKALIZING ALMOND MILK KEFIR is a little closer in appearance and mouthfeel to the original, centuries-old dairy version. It's absolutely delicious and perfect as a base for a cultured Moon Milk.

This is also a great way to preserve a batch of nut or seed milk that you won't be able to get through before the bad bacteria gets to it. Rather than letting it spoil or freezing it, explore a nut milk kefir.

ALMOND MILK KEFIR

MAKES 16 OUNCES

PROBIOTIC

IMMUNITY FOOD

BEAUTY FOOD

16 ounces Almond Milk (page 100)
½ teaspoon probiotic
Liquid stevia (optional)

Pour the almond milk into a 1-quart glass jar and use a wooden spoon or a straw to stir in the probiotics. Cover the opening of the jar with a nut milk bag, cheesecloth, or piece of cotton and secure it with a rubber band. Let stand on the counter (or on top of your running dehydrator if your kitchen is very cool) until the kefir has separated into cream on top, with a yellowish-clear water on the bottom. This may happen in as little as 8 hours if the room is warm, or as long as overnight.

Stir vigorously with a spoon to recombine. Serve plain or sweetened with stevia. Drink immediately or store the kefir in the refrigerator for up to several days.

I LOVE THIS ANCIENT AYURVEDIC, system-balancing drink, but am too sensitive to cow's milk to indulge in traditional mango lassis. I created our probiotic coconut yoghurt alternative to reach an even deeper level of healing and pleasure. It's one of my favorite snacks in warmer months because it is incredibly cooling, and a true beauty food. Bioavailable and system-cleansing probiotics support the skin and gut. Mango is a blood builder, and coconut nourishes the thyroid.

PROBIOTIC MANGO LASSI

MAKES 16 OUNCES

PROBIOTIC

BEAUTY FOOD

DIGESTIVE AID

¾ cup chopped fresh mango (from ¾ mango)
½ cup fresh coconut meat
Zest and juice of ½ juicy lime
1 teaspoon raw honey, or 1 drop of stevia
Pinch of pink salt
1 cup water
1 teaspoon probiotic

Combine the mango, coconut meat, lime juice, honey, salt, and water in a blender. Blend on high until creamy and smooth with a pourable, yoghurtlike texture. Transfer to a jar and use a wooden spoon or straw to stir in the probiotics. (The heat from blending will give you a slightly warmed lassi that will receive the probiotic very well.) For a tangier drink, let the lassi ferment on the counter for a couple of hours; otherwise, garnish with the lime zest and drink it immediately or store it in the fridge for up to several days.

CHEESES

I eat a cheese and crisp sandwich almost every day. I hate to sound so predictable, but unless I'm out on the town, some version of a cheese sandwich and a cultured vegetable salad is my lunch. There are days when I realize everything I've eaten has some form of cheese in it, from sprouted toast with cashew cheese, sea salt, and honey, to quinoa macaroni and cheese for my son.

The wonderful thing about cheeses made from the Moon Pantry is that a mother batch can last you three months or longer. I generally make a giant batch of cashew–macadamia nut cheese with no salt to use as the basis of cured cheeses, desserts, or spreads as the spirit moves me. When I make cheese, I have a little ritual of "washing" the blender out with 6 to 8 ounces of water after removing as much of the puree as possible with a rubber spatula to make macadamia milk. You can never get fully into the blades, so this is a great way to use every last bit, which I save for a chocolate shake.

THIS IS THE BASIC CHEESE I create in volume, doubling or even tripling the recipe each time I make it. I don't add any salt or flavorings to allow for maximum flexibility. I let my cheese stand on the counter for a couple of days before I refrigerate it because I like it really tangy. For a milder cheese more like a farmer's cheese or pot cheese, refrigerate it immediately. You can also pack the cheese into a ring mold and dehydrate it for a firmer cheese.

One of my favorite ways to dress this up is by adding lots of herbs and shallots. It brings to mind lazy afternoons in southern France spent outside with tapenade, and soft herbed goat cheese.

SOFT CHEESE BASE

MAKES 2½ CUPS

1½ cups raw cashews
1 cup raw macadamia nuts
1 cup water
½ teaspoon probiotic

In separate bowls, soak the cashews and macadamia nuts in water to cover overnight. The next day, drain and rinse the nuts and transfer both to a blender. Add the water and blend until smooth. Transfer to a 1-quart glass jar and use a wooden spoon or straw to mix in the probiotics until thoroughly incorporated.

Incubate for 24 hours in your dehydrator at 85°F to 90°F if it goes that low; otherwise, set the jar on top of your stove with the oven set to low. Allow the cheese base to ferment at room temperature for 48 hours.

Store in the refrigerator until ready to serve.

VARIATION: SOFT HERB & SHALLOT CHEESE
Fold in 2 tablespoons chopped shallots, 1 teaspoon chopped fresh chives, 1½ teaspoons minced fresh tarragon, 2 teaspoons chopped fresh parsley, 1 teaspoon pink salt, ½ teaspoon freshly ground black pepper, and ½ teaspoon fresh lemon juice into 2½ cups of cheese base. Use as is as a spread or pack into a small ring mold and dehydrate for 12 hours. Unmold the cheese and flip it upside down on the dehydrator sheet. Dehydrate for an additional 24 hours.

PLANT PROTEIN

DIGESTIVE AID

BEAUTY FOOD

THIS CHEESE is an elegant expression of the stunning complexity of the Hawaiian macadamia nut. It's not often that you get to enjoy a savory macadamia nut. This simple farm cheese is versatile and soft, and can be used any way you use cheese. I like it for breakfast on warm sprouted toast with sea salt and raw honey.

I make this monthly, tripling the recipe so I always have a good quantity on hand.

PLANT
PROTEIN

DIGESTIVE
AID

BEAUTY
FOOD

CURED MACADAMIA NUT CHEESE

MAKES 2 CUPS

1¾ cups raw cashews
1 cup raw macadamia nuts
⅓ cup water
2 tablespoons pink salt
½ teaspoon probiotic

In separate bowls, soak the cashews and macadamia nuts in water to cover overnight. The next day, drain and rinse the nuts and transfer both to a blender. Add the water, and salt and blend until smooth. Transfer the cheese base to a 1-quart glass jar and add the probiotic with a wooden spoon or straw, stirring until it is thoroughly incorporated.

Incubate for 24 hours in your dehydrator at 85ºF to 90ºF if it goes that low; otherwise, set the jar on top of your stove with the oven on its lowest setting; it should be just warm to the touch. Allow the cheese base to ferment at room temperature for 48 hours.

Pipe the cheese into molds and freeze for 1 to 2 hours. Push the cheese out of the molds directly onto dehydrator sheets, and dehydrate at 118ºF for 12 hours. Flip the cheese molds and dehydrate for an additional 24 hours.

CHAPTER 7

FERMENTED VEGETABLES

Another important source of valuable probiotics and good bacteria is fermented vegetables. You can ferment just one vegetable or a mixture. Almost any local, farm-fresh produce can be fermented with just an airtight jar, water, and salt.

Cultured veggies can be used as a condiment with anything, as they balance flavors with an element of sour. But most important, they provide a dose of probiotics, which aid digestion and help you assimilate more of the nutrients from the food you consume. Happy gut flora leads to liver cleansing, skin glow, and improved mood.

At one time I struggled with a refined sugar and bread addiction. I couldn't figure out an effective way to stay away from these vices. The thing that really changed my experience and my life was fermented foods—in particular, cultured vegetables. Every time I felt a sugar craving or a sugar detox freak-out—headaches, bad moods, pimples, and itching—fermented foods were my go-to. It took some willpower to choose cultured vegetables instead of cake, but having vats of home-made ferments in my kitchen made the whole thing possible. They were something I could pack up and travel with, but make at home whenever I wanted.

I've now been eating cultured veggies daily for more than a decade, and they've allowed me to stay on track. I've noticed a huge difference in my skin, mood, sleep cycles, hormonal balance, ability to digest, and capacity to enjoy foods that are not on my daily go-to list. Because I've built a strong gut and have these veggies to fall back on daily, I can make certain allowances for foods that I could barely tolerate before.

I've gone through some wild and stinky adventures in the kitchen to come up with my favorite cultured veggie formulas and to discover the cleanest method for their preparation. After a few tries, you will see how easy it is to develop a relationship with the fermentation process. Like playing an instrument or having a houseplant, this is a moving, growing relationship that you can play with, alter, speed up, or slow down.

It is important to get in tune with how your environment is affecting fermentation. Colder weather will slow down the process, while a warmer spot in the kitchen may speed it up. Everyone's fermentation will be different because your blend may include bacteria that are natural and specific to your environment.

Jars of fermented veggies make great gifts, and making them in big batches can turn into a really fun crafting night with friends. They are perfect to eat on their own or alongside cooked foods for flavor. Add any of these ferments to olive oil for a delicious dressing for salads and veggies.

PICKLES

Where cultured vegetables get their sour taste from the fermentation process, pickles get their sour taste from an acid, like citrus or vinegar. And while cultured vegetables can take weeks to prepare, quick pickles are ready in just a few hours.

These quick pickles have the bold crunch of a raw vegetable, but have been chemically broken and had their flavors condensed, enhanced, and teased out. I love these pickles in a salad, running with the fresh crunch theme, or as a great addition to cooked foods that need a bright and fresh juxtaposition.

Each of these pickles creates a colorful and decadent juice. Depending on how you use them, you'll need to store them submerged in the liquid. If you're using all the pickles, the juice makes for a great salad dressing or sauce for a bowl.

DAVID TANIS, a chef at Chez Panisse for more than twenty years, inspired the flavor combination for this recipe. One day when I was at the restaurant I went into the kitchen to say hello, and as we stood talking he speared a piece of fennel and green apple on a toothpick, added a little crushed juniper berry and a squeeze of lemon, and gave it to me.

I thought it was one of the smartest flavor profiles I'd ever tasted. It was so intriguing and complex that I thought about it for years. I tried scaling it up as a salad, but the juniper was too overbearing.

It wasn't until I started culturing veggies that I found a perfect way to use these ingredients. The fermentation process only enhanced the flavor combination, as the resulting sourness was able to stand up to the juniper. Juniper berries are extremely good for the kidneys, but they have a particular taste. It can be difficult to find a way to enjoy them outside of a more traditional pairing like duck.

This recipe is a great way to get down with juniper berries. Keep a jar in your fridge and eat it on its own, or throw it into salads and bowls.

CULTURED FENNEL, APPLE & JUNIPER

PROBIOTIC

BEAUTY FOOD

MAKES THREE 1½-QUART JARS

2 medium green cabbages, 3 outer leaves reserved, the rest shredded in a food processor

1½ green apples, cored and thinly sliced by hand or on a mandoline

1 medium fennel bulb, shredded in a food processor

2 teaspoons fennel seeds

2 teaspoons juniper berries

Pink salt to taste

In a large bowl, combine all the ingredients except the 3 reserved cabbage leaves and the salt. Remove 3 cups of the mixture and transfer to a blender with ½ cup water. Blend on high until the mixture has the consistency of a thick juice. Pour the blended mixture back into the bowl and mix it with the shredded vegetables to coat them evenly.

Transfer the mixture to three 1½-quart sterilized glass jars or stainless-steel containers. Use your fist to pack the veggies tightly, leaving a few inches of space at the top for the veggies to expand. Depending on the size of your cabbages and how tightly you pack them, you may not fill all three jars, which is fine.

Roll up the reserved whole cabbage leaves into a tight "cigarillo" and place them in the jars to fill the remaining space.

Screw on the lids.

Let the veggies stand at room temperature for at least 3 days—a week is even better. If your kitchen is cooler than 70°F, place the jars on top of an operating dehydrator to create a warmer environment. When the vegetables have fermented to your liking, add a bit of salt to slow down any further fermentation and place the jars in the refrigerator. In a covered container, they will keep for a month or more.

HIJIKI, SCALLION, AND GINGER ENRICH the tang of naturally cultured cabbage and carrot. The natural sugars from shaved carrot feed probiotic bacteria, while the hijiki mineralizes and nourishes the thyroid with its iodine.

This is a great way to start incorporating sea vegetables into your daily diet, as hijiki has a mild flavor that goes beautifully with the rest of the ferment. It's so delicious that I often eat a bowl of it on its own, topped with avocado and drizzled with olive oil.

CULTURED SEA VEGETABLES

PROBIOTIC

HORMONE
BALANCER

MAKES THREE 1½-QUART JARS

2 cups shredded green cabbage
  plus 9 large outer leaves
1 cup shredded carrot
½ cup grated fresh ginger
1 cup hijiki
1 cup sliced scallions
1 teaspoon probiotic
½ cup water
Pink salt to taste

In a large bowl, combine all the ingredients except the water cabbage leaves and salt. Transfer 3 cups of the mixture to a blender along with the water. Blend on high until the mixture has the consistency of a thick juice. Return the blended mixture to the bowl and mix it with the shredded vegetables, stirring well.

Transfer the mixture to three sterilized 1½-quart glass jars or stainless-steel containers. Use your fist to pack the veggies tightly, leaving a few inches of space at the tops of the jars for the veggies to expand.

Roll up the reserved whole cabbage leaves into a tight "cigarillo" and place them in the jar to fill the remaining space. Screw on the lids.

Let the veggies stand at room temperature for at least 3 days—a week is even better. If your kitchen is cooler than 70°F, place the jar on top of an operating dehydrator to create a warmer environment. When the vegetables have fermented to your liking, add a bit of salt to slow down any further fermentation and place the jars in the refrigerator. In a covered container they will keep for a month or more.

THIS IS THE green fantasy blend of every cleansing, nourishing, powerhouse element I most covet. Dandelion and burdock deeply cleanse the liver, nettles nourish the blood, and daikon enhances the natural probiotic content. Jalapeño warms and moves the blood as juicy limes alkalize and polish the blend. This ferment is right up there with my green juice in terms of being a daily staple.

SPICY CULTURED GREEN VEGGIES

MAKES THREE 1½-QUART JARS

PROBIOTIC

DETOXIFIER

2 medium green cabbages,
   9 outer leaves reserved,
   the rest shredded in a food
   processor
2 cups shredded fresh burdock
2 cups thinly sliced daikon
2 cups sliced dandelion greens
   (sliced ½ inch thick on an angle)
1 teaspoon probiotic
Juice of 2 limes
2 cups nettle leaves, or 2 tablespoons nettle leaf extract
3 jalapeños, seeded and minced
½ cup water
Pink salt to taste

In a large bowl, combine all the ingredients except the whole cabbage leaves, the water, and the salt. Transfer 3 cups of the mixture to a blender along with the water and blend on high until pureed. Return to the bowl and mix with the shredded vegetables, stirring well.

Transfer the mixture to three sterilized 1½-quart glass jars or stainless-steel containers. Use your fist to pack the veggies tightly, leaving a few inches of space at the tops of the jars for the veggies to expand.

Roll up the reserved whole cabbage leaves into tight "cigarillos" and place them in the jars to fill the remaining space. Screw on the lids.

Let the veggies stand at room temperature for at least 3 days— a week is even better. If your kitchen is cooler than 70°F, place the jars on top of an operating dehydrator to create a warmer environment. When the vegetables have fermented, add a bit of salt to slow down any further fermentation and place the jars in the refrigerator. In a covered container, they will keep for 1 month or more.

APPLE CIDER VINEGAR is incredible for gut health and alkalization, and turmeric helps the body process fat while acting as a powerful anti-inflammatory, liver support, blood cleanser, and overall wonder root. This is quite the beautifying pickle.

Turmeric stands up nicely to ghee and other fats, so it's great paired with heavier meals. It's just the thing to serve alongside rich curries. I also love little slivers of it buried in an avocado wrap or to spice up a grain bowl.

My favorite part may be the garlic juice it creates. Mixed with olive oil it's a perfect dressing and you can sip on it straight as an immunity shot or digestion tonic. Not gonna lie, though: Your hands will get stained with golden turmeric—think of them as battle scars from pickle making!

TURMERIC CIDER PICKLES

MAKES A MONTH'S SUPPLY, OR ENOUGH FOR 15 PEOPLE

INFLAMMATION
TAMER

IMMUNITY
FOOD

1 (3-ounce) piece fresh turmeric
    root
3 cloves garlic, smashed with the
    side of a knife
3 chiles de àrbol, torn in thirds
    by hand
½ teaspoon pink salt
½ cup apple cider vinegar

Scrape the peel from the turmeric root with the side of a spoon and then use a mandoline to slice it lengthwise into long, thin strips. Place the sliced turmeric in a clean 1-quart glass jar and add the garlic, chiles, salt, and vinegar. Cover and refrigerate for up to a month, and use as soon as an hour later.

CHAPTER 8

COSMIC PROVISIONS

My journey to live plant foods began as meditations on the perfection of fruits and vegetables from the farmers' market and the highest-quality nuts and seeds I could find. After years of appreciating these foods in their simple states, I began to play with them, respecting their inherent intelligence and beauty while entertaining my natural inclination to organize and reorganize their perfection.

This collection of foods represents the building blocks of your Moon Kitchen. All savory and sweet Cosmic Provisions are made from 100 percent organic, raw, and activated ingredients. Stocking your fridge and pantry with these nutrient-dense, enzymatically live, extraordinarily mineral-rich, and easy-to-digest foods will catapult you into a whole new system of eating and preparing live foods. Most take just seconds to prepare, and, combined with the produce you have on hand, will inspire many meals and satisfy your body's wildest snacking needs.

FOR YEARS, I ate oatmeal every morning to fuel my day. Oats are an incredible example of plant fuel, yet they always seemed to have the opposite effect on me. I've since learned that when you cook oats, they become acidic, while raw oats are very gentle and alkalizing on the system.

To serve this muesli, I soak the oat mixture in pumpkin seed milk overnight, an effortless way to bring out the natural creaminess of oats and provide decadence because the heavy lifting of this recipe is done while you sleep. You can easily scale this up or down to serve one or ten.

White mulberries and maple syrup are mineral dense, while the pumpkin seeds and pumpkin milk are hormone regulating and libido boosting.

MOON MUESLI

MINERALIZES
DEEPLY

ENERGY
FOOD

MAKES 15 CUPS

11½ cups rolled oats
1½ cups unsweetened coconut
    flakes
2 cups dried mulberries
2 cups raw pumpkin seeds
1 teaspoon pink salt
2 tablespoons plus 1 teaspoon
    chia seeds
½ teaspoon freshly grated nutmeg
1 tablespoon ground cinnamon
1 cup pure maple syrup

In a large bowl, whisk together all the ingredients except the maple syrup to blend thoroughly. Drizzle with the maple syrup and toss with a rubber spatula to coat evenly.

Spread the mixture evenly on dehydrator sheets and dehydrate at 118°F or the closest setting on your dehydrator for 24 hours. Transfer to an airtight container and store at room temperature for up to 3 months.

To serve, stir 1 cup of the muesli with 2 cups Pumpkin Seed Milk (page 101). Refrigerate overnight; in the morning your overnight oats will be ready to go! Garnish with sprouted pumpkin seeds.

I HAVE A DIE-HARD LOVE OF GRANOLA, but eventually it hit me that it was basically crumbled cookies. It was a grim couple of years until I devised an empowering, nourishing, enzymatically potent granola—that still tastes that good.

Pair this granola with any nut milk you prefer for breakfast. Its flavor is so exceptional, you'll want to eat it by the fistful. You can also form it into a granola bar shape prior to dehydrating for easy snacking on the go.

SALTED MAPLE REISHI GRANOLA

MAKES 18 CUPS

BRAIN ACTIVATOR

IMMUNITY FOOD

1¼ cups almond butter
5 cups pure maple syrup
1¼ cups activated almonds
5 cups activated buckwheat
2 cups activated rolled oats
2 cups activated golden flaxseed
1 cup activated sunflower seeds
1 cup activated pumpkin seeds
⅔ cup water
5 teaspoons reishi powder
1 tablespoon ground cinnamon
2 teaspoons pink salt

In a blender, combine the almond butter and maple syrup and blend until smooth. Pulse the almonds in a food processor until just coarsely chopped. Transfer the almonds to a large bowl and add the buckwheat, oats, flaxseed, sunflower seeds, pumpkin seeds, water, reishi, cinnamon, and salt. Mix well, then pour the blended almond butter and maple syrup into the bowl and use a rubber spatula to fold and massage the ingredients together until evenly incorporated. Set aside one-third of the mixture and transfer the remainder to the food processor. Pulse a few times, then return to the bowl with the unchopped portion and knead by hand until well blended. Using dampened hands, press the dough onto a dehydrator sheet to about ⅛-inch thickness, packing it firmly, evenly, and tightly. Dehydrate at 118°F or the closest setting on your dehydrator for 5 hours. Break the sheet of granola into bite-size pieces, then continue to dehydrate for 7 hours more, or until dry. Let cool and store in an airtight container at room temperature for up to 3 months.

MY FAVORITE CHILDHOOD SNACK FOOD was salt-and-vinegar potato chips. The more I took care of my body, though, the less they appealed to me. Dulse & Vinegar Almonds are my version of the salt-and-vinegar chip experience—one that my body can appreciate.

I try to incorporate as much seaweed into my diet as I can to support my thyroid, and the dulse in this recipe provides salinity and healing iodine. Apple cider vinegar is not only delicious but also good for the gut. When the almonds are marinated in this mixture and then dehydrated, they have an almost shattered glass crispness that fried food can only dream of.

DULSE & VINEGAR ALMONDS

PROBIOTIC

MINERALIZES DEEPLY

MAKES 4 CUPS

4 cups raw almonds
2 cups apple cider vinegar, plus
    more as needed
3 tablespoons liquid aminos
3 tablespoons dulse flakes
1 teaspoon pink salt
3 tablespoons shiitake mushroom
    powder

Place the almonds in a bowl and cover with the apple cider vinegar, adding more if needed to fully submerge them. Soak for 8 hours or overnight. Strain the almonds, reserving the vinegar separately to reuse for salad or any other recipes that call for vinegar.

Return the almonds to the bowl and add the liquid aminos, dulse, salt, and shiitake powder and toss to coat the nuts evenly. Transfer the almonds to a dehydrator, spreading them evenly in a single layer. Be sure to scrape out any seasoning left in the bowl using a rubber spatula and mix it with the nuts. Dehydrate at 105°F or the closest setting on your dehydrator for 24 hours. Stored in an airtight container at room temperature, the nuts will keep indefinitely.

THIS SAVORY, TANGY, activated seed mix was created as a very potent anti-inflammatory, using the inflammation-taming properties of turmeric, coconut, and pumpkin seeds. When these three ingredients are balanced with a good deal of lime juice and a hint of chile, they become one of the tastiest snack foods you'll ever taste. It's a bright, fresh seed salad, not heavy as many nut mixes can be.

I make a large batch of this quarterly.

INFLAMMATION TAMER

HORMONE BALANCER

TURMERIC, COCONUT & LIME PEPITAS

MAKES 4½ CUPS

4 cups pumpkin seeds
½ cup unsweetened shaved
    coconut
6 tablespoons fresh young
    coconut meat
4 teaspoons ground turmeric
4 teaspoons curry powder
6 chiles de árbol, **seeded**
2 teaspoons pink salt
4 teaspoons fresh lime juice

Soak the pumpkin seeds in water to cover overnight. The next day, drain the seeds and place them in a bowl along with the shaved coconut. In a blender, combine the coconut meat, turmeric, curry powder, chiles, salt, and lime juice.

Blend until the coconut meat is fully pureed. Add to the bowl with the pumpkin seeds and shaved coconut. Stir until the pumpkin seeds are evenly coated with the marinade.

Spread evenly in a single layer on the dehydrator sheet. Dehydrate at 118°F or the closest setting on your dehydrator until crunchy, 24 to 36 hours. The pepitas will naturally break apart as you transfer them to a resealable plastic bag or airtight container, but it's nice to leave some clusters for snacking. Stored in an airtight container at room temperature, these will keep for up to 3 months.

I FIRST MADE THESE BUNDLES because I love nut brittle and caramel turtles, and wanted to create an alternative that would actually be useful to my system. After many an interesting experiment, I locked on to this combination of sprouted walnuts covered in a caramel concoction of maca, mesquite, cinnamon, and banana, and slow dried to a toffee crunch.

Not only is it delicious, but it's high functioning and energizing, with activated walnuts to feed the brain and stimulating maca.

MACA MESQUITE WALNUTS

BRAIN
ACTIVATOR

ENERGY
FOOD

MAKES 4½ CUPS

8 Medjool dates, pitted
3 large, ripe bananas
1 cup water
5 tablespoons maple syrup
5 teaspoons mesquite powder
5 teaspoons maca powder
1 teaspoon raw vanilla bean
    powder
1 tablespoon ground cinnamon
1 tablespoon almond butter
1½ teaspoons pink salt
4 cups activated walnuts

Put the dates in a bowl and add warm water to cover. Soak for at least 20 minutes, then drain. Transfer the dates to a blender and add the remaining ingredients except the walnuts. Blend until well combined. Place the walnuts in a bowl, add the blended mixture, and toss to coat.

Transfer the mixture to a dehydrator sheet, allowing it to form small clumps. Dehydrate at 118°F or the closest setting on your dehydrator for 24 hours or until completely dried (it will still feel sticky when warm). Let cool. Stored in an airtight container at room temperature, the nuts will keep for up to 3 months.

THIS RECIPE STARTED as a bag of hazelnuts, mulberries, and cacao nibs that I put together from the bulk foods section at the grocery store and carried with me throughout my day. I loved the flavor combination and the energy it gave me: a healthy, raw version of a Cadbury Dairy Milk Fruit and Nut bar. Uniting the flavors with a hit of pink salt and a touch of coconut nectar to bind the broken mulberries, I realized my ultimate fantasy snack food.

Mulberries are deeply mineralizing, hazelnuts provide alkalizing plant protein, and the cacao is brain and energy food.

HAZELNUT CRUNCHERS

MAKES 4½ CUPS

4 cups hazelnuts
½ cup mulberries
¼ cup cacao nibs
¾ cup yacón syrup
1 teaspoon pink salt

Soak the hazelnuts in water to cover overnight. The next day, drain the nuts and place them in a medium bowl. Pulse the mulberries in a food processor briefly, then add them to the bowl with the nuts. Add the cacao nibs, yacón syrup, and salt and toss to coat evenly. Spread the mixture on a dehydrator sheet and dehydrate for 12 hours at 118°F or the closest setting on your dehydrator. Break the mixture into small clumps and continue to dehydrate for 24 hours or until the hazelnuts have a candied nutlike texture. Let cool. Stored in an airtight container at room temperature, these will keep for up to 3 months.

BRAIN
ACTIVATOR

ENERGY
FOOD

THESE JERKYLIKE STRIPS are pops of intense, savory, gamey flavor that can be eaten on their own or used to accentuate a wrap, sweet potato, cheese plate, or salad. The natural meatiness of the mushroom, when dehydrated, becomes concentrated and powerful enough to hold its own against the intensely herbal rosemary. The tips are very easy to make and are so flavorful that you can use them as a condiment, as you might use bacon to add an umami punch to an avocado sandwich.

REISHI AND ROSEMARY PORTOBELLO TIPS

MAKES 1 CUP

BRAIN ACTIVATOR

IMMUNITY FOOD

¼ cup nama shoyu (raw soy sauce)
2 tablespoons extra-virgin olive oil
¼ cup chopped onion
¼ cup finely chopped fresh parsley
2 tablespoons nutritional yeast
1 tablespoon freshly ground black pepper
1 tablespoon minced garlic
1 teaspoon finely chopped fresh rosemary
1 teaspoon cayenne
½ teaspoon reishi powder
4 or 5 medium portobello mushroom caps, sliced
½ zucchini, cut on a mandoline into thin rounds

In a small bowl, whisk together the nama shoyu, olive oil, onion, parsley, nutritional yeast, black pepper, garlic, rosemary, cayenne, and reishi. In a large bowl, combine the mushrooms and zucchini. Pour the seasoning mixture over the vegetables and toss to coat, gently squeezing the mushrooms to massage the seasonings into them. Set aside to marinate for 10 to 15 minutes, squeezing the mushrooms occasionally to help incorporate the marinade.

Spread the vegetables on a dehydrator sheet and dehydrate at 118°F or the closest setting on your dehydrator for 4 hours. Stir and dehydrate for 12 hours more, until the mushrooms have a jerky-like consistency. Store in a tightly sealed, airtight container at room temperature for up to 1 month.

THE KEY TO THIS RECIPE'S SUCCESS is sourcing truly vibrant dried mango. Look for a beautiful orange color, an intense mango smell, and complex flavor notes. It shouldn't be just sweet—you should actually be able to taste the aroma of the mango.

Accentuated with lime and a good shake of chile, this snack is blood-nourishing, addictive, and fiber-rich. It's everything that's great about a Mexican fruit stand.

CHILE & LIME MANGO

MAKES 4 CUPS

4 cups dried mango
1 cup fresh lime juice
1 teaspoon ground chipotle chile
1 teaspoon pink salt

Combine all the ingredients in a large bowl and toss until the mango is evenly coated. Let the mango absorb the lime juice.

Spread the mixture on a dehydrator sheet in a single layer. Dehydrate at 118°F or the closest setting on your dehydrator for 4 hours. The mango should be dried but sticky and a little chewy. Store in an airtight container for up to 3 months.

ENERGY
FOOD

METABOLISM
BOOSTER

THE SLIGHTLY SWEET, toothsome texture of papaya is the perfect platform for the beautifying schisandra berry and earthy, mineralizing cacao.

SCHISANDRA PAPAYA

MAKES ½ POUND

3 tablespoons cacao powder

1¼ teaspoons ground cinnamon

¾ teaspoon ground schisandra berries

½ cup warm water

½ pound dried papaya

DIGESTIVE AID

BEAUTY FOOD

In a bowl, combine the cacao, cinnamon, schisandra, and water; whisk together thoroughly. Add the papaya and toss to coat. Set aside for 30 minutes.

Arrange the papaya on a dehydrator sheet and dehydrate at 118°F or the closest setting on your dehydrator for 2 hours, or until the papaya is heavily coated and the marinade does not come off on your hands. The papaya will have a softly chewy, jerky texture. Store in an airtight container for up to 3 months.

I LOVE TO CUT these eggplant slices into small pieces to tuck into a wrap sandwich or slice them to mix into a salad. The slices also make a nice base for a canapé of avocado and cultured veggies.

EGGPLANT ZA'ATAR

MAKES 12 SLICES

1 medium eggplant
1 teaspoon pink salt
¼ cup water
¼ cup sesame butter
2 tablespoons olive oil
1 clove garlic
Juice of ½ lemon
2 tablespoons za'atar

ENERGY
FOOD

MINERALIZES
DEEPLY

Slice the eggplant lengthwise about ½ inch thick. You should end up with about 12 slices.

Score the eggplant slices lightly on one side with the tip of a knife (do not slice all the way through). Salt the slices evenly, which will draw out the eggplant's bitter juices. Let sit for at least 30 minutes, then use a paper towel to dab off any accumulated liquid.

Meanwhile, in a blender, combine the water, sesame butter, olive oil, garlic, and lemon juice and blend until smooth. Pour the mixture into a shallow bowl and stir in the za'atar. Dredge the eggplant slices in the sesame butter mixture and lay them on dehydrator sheets. Dehydrate at 118°F or the closest setting on your dehydrator for 6 hours, or until the slices have a firm, jerkylike texture. For a crisper eggplant chip, dehydrate an additional 5 hours or so. Store in an airtight container for up to 3 months.

WRAPS AND OPEN-FACED CRISP SANDWICHES

Don't think of wraps as a dainty, tedious affair. You will surprise yourself at how much you can fit into a wrap and how many you can eat at once. When I started ensuring I had all the necessary ingredients for wraps on hand, it was really a breakthrough moment that showed me how easy it is to eat this way; I could simply reach into the fridge and pull out leaves, fillings, and flavorings, and wrap up a nearly instant meal anytime.

A wrap should include something fatty and yummy like a cheese, avocado, savory tomato jam, hummus, or a veggie puree or savory yoghurt; a cultured veggie or pickle; and fresh herbs. For wrapping, try using collard green or Swiss chard leaves with the rib trimmed out, nori sheets, a butter lettuce cup, a napa cabbage leaf, Treviso, endive, romaine; any spiny lettuce turns more into a taco than a wrap or a burrito, but it's the same idea. If I'm using nori as the wrapper, I like to add some shredded lettuce or microgreens. I often keep baked sweet potatoes or winter squash on hand. They keep for days in the fridge and a few tablespoons squished into the wrap really fortifies it. Two or three of these make an incredible "fast food" lunch. Any of these combinations can be built on one of the crisps on page 194 for an open-faced sandwich.

On the following page are a few combinations I return to again and again. It should go without saying that the wrap fillings could easily be used as crisp toppings, and vice versa.

WRAPS

CULTURED SEA VEGETABLES
ume paste, sliced daikon, greens, avocado, wrapped in nori

SUMAC TOMATO JAM WITH PINE NUTS
Cured Macadamia Nut Cheese, basil, in a stemmed collard leaf

THINLY SLICED KELP RIBBONS
Shallot & Mint Raita, quick-pickled carrot, wrapped in a lettuce leaf

HUMMUS
pickles, raw black olives, mint, wrapped in a stemmed dinosaur kale leaf

COCONUT YOGHURT
with dill, walnuts, and herbs, radish salad, lemon, wrapped in a napa cabbage leaf

RAW HERB & CHEESE DOUGH
Spicy Cultured Green Veggies, wrapped in a stemmed Swiss chard leaf

CRISPS

FERMENTED GREEN CRISPS
with Cured Macadamia Nut Cheese and Cultured Green Veggies

FERMENTED GREEN CRISPS
with avocado and Turmeric Cider Pickles

CUMIN & CHARD CRISPS
with Cured Macadamia Nut Cheese and Cultured Fennel, Apple & Juniper

BEET AID JUICE & SEED CRISPS
with hummus, Coconut Yoghurt, dill, and strips of Eggplant Za'atar

HERB & CHEESE CRISPS
with Cured Macadamia Nut Cheese, Portobello Tips, shallot, herbs, and arugula

GOODNESS GREEN JUICE AND SEED CRACKER
tomato, avocado, red onion, and dulse

THESE CRISPS and those that follow are made with activated seeds and Moon Juices. They are radiant, cosmic, spellbinding raw crackers that incorporate everything I love that comes from the earth: vegetable juices and activated seeds. These crackers are so satiating, filled with activated seed power and enzymatically potent, nutrient-dense juices that three or four will speak to many of the body's systems all at once, curbing hunger and delivering the goods.

You can soak all the seeds together in one bowl, using the ingredient with the longest soaking time as your guide for timing. The oats don't need soaking.

BEET AID JUICE & SEED CRISPS

MAKES 24 CRISPS

1¾ cups rolled oats
1¼ cups activated sunflower seeds
1 cup activated pumpkin seeds
¼ cup activated chia seeds
¼ cup activated poppy seeds
⅓ cup activated flaxseeds
1 cup beet juice pulp
½ cup fresh lemon juice
½ cup extra-virgin olive oil
2 tablespoons psyllium husks
2 tablespoons fresh beet juice
4 teaspoons pink salt
4 cups water

Combine the oats and seeds in a large bowl and mix well. In a blender, combine ½ cup of the beet pulp, the lemon juice, olive oil, psyllium husks, beet juice, and salt and puree until smooth. Add to the oats and seeds, remaining ½ cup beet pulp, and water and mix well. Set aside for 30 minutes.

Spread the dough on three dehydrator sheets in thin even layers. Dehydrate at 118°F or the closest setting on your dehydrator for 4 hours, until the dough is dry enough to lift off the dehydrator sheet. Flip the crackers and place them directly on the dehydrator rack without the dehydrator sheet for 1 hour. Cut the crackers into rectangles roughly 4 x 3 inches, then cut those in half on an angle. Return the crackers to the dehydrator for 24 hours or until completely dry and crisp. Let cool, then store in an airtight container at room temperature for up to 3 months.

ENERGY FOOD

PLANT PROTEIN

I TAKE THESE ON ROAD TRIPS or on airplanes. Eating one of these crisps with a glass of water is virtually the equivalent of drinking a big glass of green juice and eating a handful of seeds. Topped with a bit of smashed avocado, shallot or red onion, sliced tomato, lots of olive oil, salt and pepper, and topped with dulse flakes, it's one of my favorite sandwiches, my version of a BLT. The umami of the tomato and dulse paired with the luscious fats of the avocado and olive oil conjure up some serious sandwich nostalgia.

GOODNESS GREEN JUICE & SEED CRACKER

MINERALIZES DEEPLY

PLANT PROTEIN

MAKES 24 CRACKERS

1¾ cups activated rolled oats
1¼ cups activated sunflower seeds
1 cup activated pumpkin seeds
¼ cup activated chia seeds
¼ cup activated poppy seeds
⅓ cup activated flaxseeds
1 cup green juice pulp
1 cup packed fresh spinach leaves
½ cup fresh lemon juice
2 tablespoons psyllium husks
4 teaspoons pink salt
½ cup extra-virgin olive oil
4 cups water

Combine the oats and seeds in a large bowl and mix well. In a blender, combine ½ cup of the green juice pulp, the spinach, lemon juice, psyllium husks, salt, and olive oil and puree until smooth. Add to the bowl with the oats and seeds, along with the remaining ½ cup green juice pulp and water and mix well. Set aside for 30 minutes.

Spread the dough on three dehydrator sheets in thin, even layers. Dehydrate at 118°F or the closest setting on your dehydrator for 4 hours, until the dough is dry enough to lift off the dehydrator sheet. Flip the crackers and place them directly on the dehydrator rack without the dehydrator sheet for 1 hour. Cut the crackers into rectangles roughly 4 x 3 inches, then cut those in half on an angle. Return the crackers to the dehydrator for 24 hours or until completely dry and crisp. Let cool, then store in an airtight container for up to 3 months.

I LOVE EXPERIMENTING with textures, spices, and flavor combinations that are more often thought of in braised or roasted dishes than in raw form. Aromatic with cumin and savory tomato, this is a lighter experience than a nut- or flax-heavy cracker.

CUMIN & CHARD CRISPS

MAKES 16 CRACKERS

2 tablespoons extra-virgin olive oil
3 cloves garlic
¼ cup chopped onion
4 teaspoons fresh lemon juice
2 Roma tomatoes
1½ teaspoons pink salt
4¼ cups water
3 tablespoons chia seeds
⅓ cup golden flaxseeds
1 cup brown flaxseeds
5 rainbow chard leaves, ribs removed, torn into 1-inch pieces
1 carrot, thinly sliced lengthwise on a mandoline
2 tablespoons smoked paprika
2 tablespoons ground cumin
Pinch of black peppercorns

In a food processor, combine the olive oil, garlic, onion, lemon juice, tomatoes, and salt and process until thoroughly combined. Add the seeds and process until most of the flaxseeds are broken, about 1 minute.

On a dehydrator sheet, combine the dough, chard leaves, and carrot slices, kneading them together with your fingers. You want to weave the chard leaves and carrot ribbons evenly throughout the dough. Start in the center of the sheet, pressing the dough outward all the way to the edges for an even ¼-inch thickness with no holes. The vegetables need this dough to bind them together, and by the end, when you have a really even dough mixture, it becomes a work of art. If you feel like a corner needs a touch of green or a gracefully curling ribbon of carrot, add one as you see fit. Combine the paprika, cumin, and peppercorns and sprinkle evenly over the dough. Dehydrate at 118°F or the closest setting on your dehydrator for 12 hours and then flip the dough and dehydrate for 12 hours more or until completely dry. Let cool, break into crackers, and store in an airtight container at room temperature for up to 3 months.

THIS IS THE PROVISION that is nearest and dearest to my heart. It's green, it's fermented, it's crispy—there's little you can't do with this versatile cracker.

These tangy crisps are made with cultured cabbage, burdock, and daikon enriched by dandelion, nettles, and jalapeño folded into a light and crunchy sprouted seed mix. I love these guys for the triple fermented sandwich—the crisps, a smear of cheese, and a dollop of fermented veggies.

FERMENTED GREEN CRISPS

MAKES 24 CRACKERS

1¼ cups flaxseeds
1¼ cups activated sunflower seeds
⅓ cup chia seeds
Juice of 1 lime
¼ onion
1 clove garlic
4 cups water
6 cups Spicy Cultured Green
    Veggies (page 169)
1 teaspoon pink salt
½ cup fresh cilantro leaves
2 jalapeños, thinly sliced on a
    mandoline (seeded for milder
    cracker)
¼ teaspoon freshly ground black
    pepper

In a blender, combine the seeds, lime juice, onion, garlic, water, and 3 cups of the cultured veggies and blend until smooth. Pour the mixture into a large bowl and add 2 cups of the cultured veggies. Mix with a rubber spatula.

Spread the mixture onto dehydrator sheets in smooth, thin layers. Top with the cilantro leaves, the remaining 1 cup cultured veggies, and the jalapeños, and sprinkle with the pepper. Lightly press the herbs and veggies into the wet dough.

Dehydrate at 118°F or the closest setting on your dehydrator for 12 hours, flip the sheets, and dehydrate for 12 hours more or until crisp. Let cool, break into crackers, and store in an airtight container at room temperature for up to 3 months.

CHAPTER 9

THE UNBAKERY

Now that you are in the swing of making your own Well Milk every week, you undoubtedly have a supply of dehydrated nut pulps in your pantry. This section includes many ways to use these nut and seed pulps to make delicious doughs. They can be part of your daily ritual because they are made of plant protein, fiber, and good raw fat rather than refined sugar and flours.

Unlike traditional pastry doughs that have one form and one function, the doughs in this book add a whole new level of freedom, creativity, and nourishment to your baking. They can be made in large batches, portioned into workable sizes—I like to make dough balls the size of a large fist—then wrapped tightly in plastic wrap and stored in the freezer for months. If I know I will be making cookies, a sweet, or a savory tart, I take a dough ball out and defrost it overnight in the fridge, where it will soften and become pliable. (To expedite the process, you can cut the partially defrosted dough and knead it with the warmth of your hands. This is what I do many mornings when my son decides he wants a breakfast character; the doughs can be worked almost like a marzipan, and on recent mornings we've made trains and snails with intricate detail. He even makes his own. Play-Doh style.) All these doughs work wonderfully as thumbprint cookies, rolled cookie dough to cut with cookie cutters, or tarts (individual-size or pressed into a 10-inch tart pan). These doughs, even when undehydrated, make for really delicious bonbons, either rolled in cacao powder or hemp seeds or, my favorite, dipped in raw chocolate. They can also be made into breakfast "crumpets," a kid favorite.

Any of the doughs can be eaten soft and raw or dehydrated and crisp. The longer you dehydrate them, the firmer and more "baked" they will become. If I want to make small apple pies with a soft dough, I may just throw them into the dehydrator for a couple of hours so that when they are ready to be served they are deliciously warm and fragrant. One of my favorite uses for the Herb & Cheese Dough on page 212 is a warm, deep dish–style pizza, which I throw back in the dehydrator just to warm. Other times I want a firmer crust and will dehydrate a large tart shell or individual tartlets until crisp.

Jams and jellies are some of my favorite sweet tools in the kitchen. But if you've ever made jam at home, you know how much white sugar goes into it. I love the idea of being able to concentrate and preserve fresh fruit flavor, but am not interested in the pounds of sugar used to achieve this. I'm happy to say there is a way to get that concentrated fresh fruit flavor and jammy texture without white sugar or even cooking. This approach uses naturally concentrated fruit sugars, pectins, and chia seeds for texture.

These jams work beautifully alongside Coconut Yoghurt in a parfait; on a sandwich; in the center of raw chocolates, pastry dough, or cookie cups; blended into nut milk; served in a bowl at brunch; stirred into chia pudding; incorporated into cakes; or dolloped over ice cream. And honestly, sometimes they're best eaten by the spoonful right out of the open fridge.

You can also spread the jam out onto your dehydrator sheet for about 12 hours and then cut and hand roll them into jelly candies. Wrap these nuggets up into waxed paper for sweet gift treats!

PASTRIES & DESSERTS

Here you'll discover some of my favorite treats and pastries, all of which are made by combining elements from The Unbakery (page 201) such as activated pastry dough, succulent jams, decadent crèmes, and raw chocolate. These recipes are the polar opposite of their traditional counterparts in every way except for the pleasure they bring. Because they are assembled from seasonal fruits and the components you have created in the Unbakery section, each of these treats is a perfectly valid vehicle for getting your daily quotient of healthy raw fats and raw foods. You can even gear your recipe to be alkalizing to the system and sneak in your daily adaptogens, too. Experiment by pulling elements from each of the categories to create decadent treats, or use some of the combinations I have suggested here. Everything in The Unbakery combines beautifully, and each element can be exported to other areas of your life. Incorporate a jam into your morning ritual. Rethink your celebratory traditions. Sweeten your daily health practice.

Choose your application: cookie, thumbprint, donut, tart or tartlet, cake or cupcake. You can use a rolling pin and cookie cutter to work with these doughs, but they do require some hands-on finesse to mold into tart shells. My preference with these doughs and really anything I can get away with in the kitchen is to forgo equipment and use my hands, so I vote for pressing the doughs out with your palms and fists to shape them into cookies, and using your thumbs to mold them into a pie form.

The height of fancy lazy expedience and ingenuity, of course, is using one of the frostings and maybe a jam or some raw chocolate, to decorate a regular cake, homemade or store bought. Although you will be consuming a bit more sugar (and it's obviously not raw) it's a good way to push your treats in a healthier direction.

APPLICATION	DOUGHS	JAMS	CRÈMES	CHOCOLATE	METHOD	DEHYDRATE
COOKIES	Any of the sweet doughs	Make cookie sandwiches with any of the sweet jams.	Make cookies sandwiches with Cashew Butter Crème or Soft Cheese Base (you can pile it on high then freeze for an ice cream sandwich).	Dip the cookies in molten chocolate; fill for sandwich cookies if you like.	Form by hand, or roll and use a cutter or knife to cut circles, squares, or triangles.	Dehydrate the cookies until firm, 10 to 12 hours.
THUMBPRINTS	Any of the sweet doughs	Fill the indentation with any of the sweet jams.	Fill with Cashew Butter Crème or Probiotic Coconut–Cream Cheese Icing	Fill with molten chocolate; refrigerate until firm.	Pinch off walnut-sized bits of dough, roll into a ball, press with your thumb to flatten and form an indentation.	If desired, to prolong shelf life, dehydrate after filling for 10 hours; dehydrate thumbprints before filling if using chocolate.
TARTS AND TARTLETS	Any dough, sweet or savory	Fill with any jam.	Top with any of the crèmes, frostings, icings, yoghurt, or soft cheese.	Spread molten chocolate in the tart shell; place in the freezer for 20 minutes, until hardened before adding another layer.	Roll out dough, fit by hand into a tart shell with removable bottom.	Dehydrate before filling for 10 hours or until firm and chewy. Select 1, 2, or 3 fillings, layering them on in any order, depending on which you want to be most visible.
CUPCAKES	Chia Sesame Dough, Carrot Gingerbread Dough	Top with any of the sweet jams.	Top with any of the crèmes.	n/a	Form ⅓ cup dough into a ball and place in a cupcake liner, leaving ½ inch of space. Top with a layer of jam and crème just crème.	n/a

THIS DOUGH DOES IT ALL: It can be pressed into tart shells, rolled into cookies, formed into donuts, and anything else your imagination conjures up. It's the perfect way to repurpose the pulp from your almond milk–making efforts. This is a wonderful dough to make cookies from, either to eat on their own or to sandwich with frosting or ice cream, or to form into cookie cups to fill with jam or chocolate. It takes well to mix-ins like cacao nibs or fresh or dried fruit, and could be spiked with an adaptogen like cordyceps. You may also choose to load the dough with fruits and nuts, protein powder, maca, or cacao, and shape it into hearty bars. I love making my own protein bars at home so I can really dictate the flavor and potency, so think about making a double or triple batch and freezing them.

VANILLA PASTRY DOUGH

MAKES 5 CUPS

1 cup activated almond flour (page 54)

1 cup activated raw almonds, finely ground in a food processor

3 cups activated oats, finely ground in a food processor

1 teaspoon raw vanilla bean powder

1 teaspoon pink salt

½ cup almond butter

1 cup pure maple syrup

Combine all the ingredients in a large bowl and mix thoroughly. Cover the dough with plastic wrap and refrigerate for 30 minutes, until it is firm. The dough is now ready to form into a tart shell or roll out to a ¼-inch thickness and cut into cookies. You may have dough left over, which you can freeze to add to your next batch, or simply make into balls and eat out of hand.

ENERGY FOOD

ALKALIZER

THIS IS AN EXQUISITE DOUGH all on its own. The apricot kernel flour really accentuates the almond flavor, making it almost like marzipan. It pairs perfectly with jams and fruit, especially stone fruits.

ALMOND PASTRY DOUGH

MAKES 4 CUPS

1 cup finely ground activated raw
    almonds
1 cup activated almond flour
    (page 54)
2 cups apricot kernel flour
    (ground apricot kernels) or
    additional ground almonds
2 teaspoons pink salt
2 teaspoons grated orange zest
¼ cup coconut sugar
¼ cup coconut oil, melted
1 cup pure maple syrup

In a medium bowl, whisk together the ground almonds, almond flour, apricot kernel flour, and salt. In a measuring cup, stir together the orange zest, coconut sugar, coconut oil, and maple syrup. Pour the wet ingredients into the bowl with the flours and mix thoroughly.

To make thumbprint cookies: Roll about 3 tablespoons of the dough into a ball. Flatten the ball between your palms, press an indentation into the center with your thumb, and place on a dehydrator sheet. Repeat with the remaining dough. Dehydrate for 24 hours at 118°F or the closest setting on your dehydrator. Store the cookies in an airtight container for up to 2 weeks.

ALKALIZER

PLANT
PROTEIN

FIGS AND SESAME SEEDS give this dough subtle and sophisticated Eastern notes. I pair it with a chaga-infused glaze to make world-class donuts (page 232).

CHIA SESAME DOUGH

MAKES 10 OUNCES

⅓ cup rolled oats
1 tablespoon sesame seeds
2 teaspoons chia seeds
½ teaspoon pink salt
½ teaspoon raw vanilla bean
  powder
¼ cup tocotrienols
½ cup Thai coconut meat
¼ cup unsweetened shredded
  coconut
2 tablespoons pure maple syrup
1 tablespoon dried Turkish figs
1½ teaspoons coconut nectar
½ teaspoon ground cinnamon
2 tablespoons psyllium husks

In a food processor, combine the oats, sesame seeds, and chia seeds and process to a fine flour. Transfer to a medium bowl and stir in the salt, vanilla, and tocotrienols.

In a blender, combine the coconut meat, shredded coconut, maple syrup, figs, coconut nectar, and cinnamon and blend until smooth; add the psyllium husks and blend for 10 seconds more. Make a well in the dry ingredients and pour the pureed mixture into the well. Stir together to form a wet dough. Roll into a ball and portion out for immediate use or divide into smaller balls to freeze for future use.

THIS MOIST AND DECADENT, not-too-sweet dough can be made by saving pulp from nut milks and vegetable juice. I like to form a batch into six small teacakes to enjoy as little snacks or afterschool treats with my son, but you could also easily use multiple batches to make a larger birthday or wedding cake.

CARROT GINGERBREAD DOUGH

MAKES 3 CUPS

1 cup rolled oats, finely ground
2 teaspoons chia seeds, finely ground
½ cup carrot juice pulp
¼ cup almond pulp (from Almond Milk, page 100)
2 tablespoons grated fresh ginger
2 tablespoons ground psyllium husks
1 teaspoon ground cinnamon
1 teaspoon ground allspice
½ teaspoon freshly grated nutmeg
¼ teaspoon ground cardamom
⅛ teaspoon raw vanilla bean powder
⅛ teaspoon pink salt
1 cup fresh carrot juice
2 tablespoons coconut oil
2½ Medjool dates, pitted and soaked in warm water for at least 20 minutes
½ cup currants

In a blender, combine the oats and chia seeds and blend on high until they are pulverized into a fine flour. Pour into a medium bowl and add the carrot and almond pulps, the ginger, psyllium husks, cinnamon, allspice, nutmeg, cardamom, vanilla, and salt. Stir to combine thoroughly.

In the blender, combine the carrot juice, coconut oil, and dates and blend to a smooth paste. Stir the carrot mixture into the dry ingredients with a rubber spatula.

Transfer the dough to a food processor and process until the dough forms a ball.

Return the dough to the mixing bowl and add the currants. Knead by hand until the currants are well incorporated. The dough is ready to use or can be divided into balls and frozen.

FOR ME, THE NINETIES could be described as one thousand and one nights of Parmesan crisps. I couldn't eat wheat, but those grain-free Parmesan crackers were delicious. When I gave up dairy, I assumed even these treats were out for me—that is, until I got hip to nutritional yeast, the delicious B-vitamin supplement that can be made to taste exactly like Parmesan cheese. My first days of loving nutritional yeast saw me whipping it into coconut oil and spreading it onto toast or sprinkling it on popcorn.

I think this versatile dough is its best iteration yet. Combined with gentle garlic, rosemary, and almond, the yeast creates a classic savory experience that delivers profound amounts of B vitamins and protein. Use it as a base for tarts and pizzas, or spread it thinly on dehydrator sheets to make crackers. Reserve some raw dough for an incredible fresh wrap filling (page 194).

HERB & CHEESE DOUGH

MAKES 5 CUPS

PLANT
PROTEIN

ENERGY
FOOD

1 clove garlic
½ shallot
1¼ cups water
2⅓ cups activated almond flour
   (page 54)
1 cup activated raw almonds,
   finely ground in food processor
⅓ cup nutritional yeast
¾ cup activated flaxseeds, finely
   ground in a blender
1 tablespoon pink salt
2 tablespoons fresh thyme leaves
1 tablespoon fresh rosemary
   leaves

In a blender, combine the garlic, shallot, and water and blend to a smoothielike consistency. In a large bowl, combine the remaining ingredients and stir to blend thoroughly. Make a well in the dry ingredients and pour the contents of the blender into the well. Mix thoroughly by hand until you have a workable wet dough. Form the dough into crackers, tart shells, or crackers, and dehydrate at 118°F or the closest setting on your dehydrator until firm or crisp, as you prefer. The dough can also be divided into balls and frozen.

THIS EXCELLENT PANTRY STAPLE is another great way to use up almond pulp from making nut milk. It can be made in about 3 minutes, stores quite well, is filled with plant proteins and fiber, and is an effortless way to add a delicious professional touch to breakfast, snacks, and desserts. You'll find countless uses for it: Sprinkle some into a yoghurt parfait, with or without your jam of choice, or crumble onto a raw chocolate tart before the chocolate sets. I love it over ice cream, and if you're looking for a sweet midnight treat and the cupboards are bare, a bowlful with hazelnut milk poured over is a great sub for cookies and milk.

Because of this streusel's raw fat content and refined mill, you can use it like a crumb crust, pressing a substantial layer into a pie tin or shallow bowl to fill with chocolate avocado mousse (or any pudding).

HAZELNUT MESQUITE STREUSEL

ALKALIZER

THYROID SUPPORT

MAKES 3 CUPS

1 cup activated hazelnuts
¾ cup activated almond flour (page 54)
½ cup coconut sugar
½ cup coconut butter
3 activated tablespoons hemp seeds
3 tablespoons mesquite powder
1 tablespoon ground cinnamon
1 teaspoon raw vanilla bean powder
¼ teaspoon pink salt

Combine all the ingredients in a blender or food processor and blend until the hazelnuts are about the size of hemp seeds.

THE GENIUS of this icing is that you can make it in big batches and store it in sealable plastic bags, so that the next time you need to whip up thirty cupcakes for the following day, your good-for-you icing is ready to go. The most fun is obviously choosing the dazzling color and flavor of your icing. Moon dust it with power foods like cordyceps, maca, cacao, or bee pollen. The variations below are really just the tip of the iceberg.

CASHEW BUTTER CRÈME

MAKES 2½ CUPS

6 ounces Lait de Coco (page 101)
½ cup coconut oil, melted
¼ cup coconut nectar
2 tablespoons sunflower lecithin
 powder
1 cup raw cashews, soaked in
 water for 4 hours and drained

In a blender, combine the Lait de Coco, coconut oil, coconut nectar, and lecithin powder and blend on high until completely smooth. With the blender running, add the cashews in small batches until they have all been incorporated, then blend until the mixture is silky smooth, about 1 minute more.

PLANT
PROTEIN

JOY
PROMOTER

VARIATIONS

CHOCOLATE REISHI BUTTER CRÈME:
2 tablespoons cacao, ¼ teaspoon cinnamon, and ½ teaspoon reishi

MINT CHIP BUTTER CRÈME:
1 teaspoon peppermint extract, 1 teaspoon matcha; garnish with 2 tablespoons cacao nibs

STRAWBERRY LUCUMA:
½ cup pureed fresh or frozen strawberries and 2 tablespoons lucuma

GOLDEN FROSTING:
1 tablespoon fresh turmeric root juice, with ¼ teaspoon ground cinnamon, and

⅛ teaspoon ground cardamom

BLUE VANILLA:
¼ teaspoon blue algae, 1 teaspoon raw vanilla powder

I CAN BOIL DOWN MY FASCINATION with sweets and sugar to one thing: icing. The scary kind that comes out of a can. This probiotic icing made with coconut and fermented cashew cheese, on the other hand, is actually good for you.

To be able to enjoy icing that's good for me, concocted with probiotics and low glycemic sweeteners, is the true definition of having your cake and eating it, too. I recommend you make extra so you can take icing shots all week long.

PROBIOTIC COCONUT-CREAM CHEESE ICING

MAKES 3½ CUPS

DIGESTIVE AID

JOY PROMOTER

2 cups Coconut Yoghurt (page 146)
½ cup coconut butter
¼ cup soaked and rinsed Irish moss (soak in a bowl of water overnight in the refrigerator then drain, rinse, and measure)
¼ cup coconut nectar
1 tablespoon vanilla extract
1 tablespoon sunflower lecithin powder
1 tablespoon fresh lemon juice
Pinch of pink salt
⅓ cup raw cashews, soaked in water for 8 hours and drained

Place all the ingredients except the cashews in a blender and blend on high until smooth. With the motor running, add the cashews in small batches until they have all been incorporated, then continue to blend until the mixture is silky smooth. Transfer to a storage container, cover, and refrigerate for 45 minutes or until firm, up to 1 week. It will thicken as it cools.

THIS IS A MOST VERSATILE ADORNMENT for your pastries, cakes, and ice cream. Fold a little bit of salt into this sweet, nutty sauce just before serving for an extra bit of sparkly crunch. You can store it in the fridge in a glass jar. Submerge the jar in warm water to loosen it to a pourable consistency.

SALTED CARAMEL SAUCE

MAKES 2½ CUPS

8 pitted Medjool dates
¼ cup raw honey or coconut
    nectar
1 cup coconut oil, melted
¼ cup almond butter
1 teaspoon raw vanilla powder
1 teaspoon pink salt

IMMUNITY
FOOD

HORMONE
BALANCER

Soak the dates in just enough warm water to cover until the dates are very soft, at least 20 minutes and up to overnight. Drain the dates, reserving the soaking liquid.

Combine the dates, honey, oil, almond butter, and vanilla in a blender. Puree on high until completely smooth, adding some of the reserved soaking liquid if too thick. Transfer the sauce to a storage container, using a rubber spatula to scrape down the sides, and store in the refrigerator for up to 5 days. Just before serving, fold in the salt.

PAIR THIS BEAUTIFUL JAM with any type of shortbread, scone, or toast and a dab of your favorite source of decadent creaminess (whether a cashew crème or clotted cream). The length of time you dehydrate it will depend on how you plan to use it; one hour will produce a fluid, preserves-like spread, while four hours in the dehydrator will result in a fruit leather–like soft candy. I sometimes mix the jam with an equal amount of yoghurt and dehydrate to make a very special cake filling, scone spread, or amazing warm yoghurt jam.

STRAWBERRY ROSE GERANIUM JAM

JOY PROMOTER

DIGESTIVE AID

MAKES 10 OUNCES

1 cup fresh or frozen strawberries
10 Medjool dates, pitted and
    soaked in water to cover for
    30 minutes
1 tablespoon fresh lemon juice
¼ teaspoon raw vanilla bean
    powder
2 drops of geranium essential oil

Combine all the ingredients in a blender and blend on high until completely smooth. Transfer to a wide-mouth jar and dehydrate at 118°F or the closest setting on your dehydrator for 1 hour for jam, 2 hours for pastry filling, and 4 hours for candy. Store jam or filling an airtight container in the refrigerator for up to 2 weeks. Candy will keep for up to 1 month in an airtight container.

SOME FRUITS CAN BE ENJOYED as much in their dried state as they are when fresh, including apricots, figs, and sour cherries. The Black Forest beauty of cherry is perfectly accentuated by the warm tones of black pepper.

CHERRY BLACK PEPPER JAM

MAKES 1½ CUPS

1 cup dried sour cherries
2 teaspoons chia seeds, ground to
   a powder in a blender
1 tablespoon fresh lemon juice
¼ teaspoon pink salt
3 grinds of a peppermill
5 drops of black pepper
   essential oil

Soak the dried cherries in warm water to cover by ½ inch for at least 20 minutes and up to a few days. Strain the soaked cherries, reserving the soaking liquid, and place them in a blender with the chia seeds, lemon juice, salt, and ground pepper. Add ½ cup of the reserved soaking liquid and puree until smooth. Add the pepper oil a drop or 2 at a time, blending after each addition. Blend until smooth or leave a few chunks of cherry for texture if you prefer. (You can also reserve a handful of dried cherries to add at the end for a very chunky texture.) Transfer to a covered container and store in the refrigerator for up to 1 week.

INFLAMMATION TAMER

IMMUNITY FOOD

THIS JAM DELIVERS a full-spectrum fig vibe, combining the iron-rich, deep dark Mission and the already jamlike, bright, sweet Turkish. There's something anciently pleasing about bringing together these two delicate fruits that have inspired hundreds of years of poetry and healing all over the planet. Persian white mulberries contribute a delicate depth of sweetness.

Because this jam uses dried fruits, its ingredients are easily accessible any time of year. The blend is deeply mineralizing, blood nourishing, and gut cleansing. It pairs well with citrus, on toast, or in a recipe. It is delicious with blood oranges and hazelnuts. If you can't find a sour orange, you could use the juice of half a small orange and half a lemon, and the zest of the orange.

Save the soaking liquid and store it in the fridge for up to a week, or freeze it in ice cube trays for a perfect sweetener. Use 1 tablespoon (or 1 ice cube) as equivalent to 1 teaspoon of any other sweetener. A tablespoon or so in sparkling water makes a fantastic probiotic soda.

FIG & MULBERRY JAM

MAKES 2 CUPS

1 cup dried Turkish figs, soaked
½ cup Mission figs
1 cup dried mulberries
6 Medjool dates
2 tablespoons chia seeds
Zest and juice of 1 small sour
     orange

Place the figs, mulberries, and dates in separate bowls with just enough warm water to cover. Soak for at least 20 minutes. If not soft enough, soften in the fridge overnight. Drain the fruits, reserving the sweet soaking liquid, (you should have about 1 cup). In a food processor, combine the dates, ¼ cup of soaking liquid, and the chia seeds and process until the dates are broken down. Add the rest of the figs and mulberries.

Transfer the mixture to a small bowl and stir in the orange zest and juice. Transfer to a covered container and refrigerate for up to 1 week.

MINERALIZES
DEEPLY

DIGESTIVE
AID

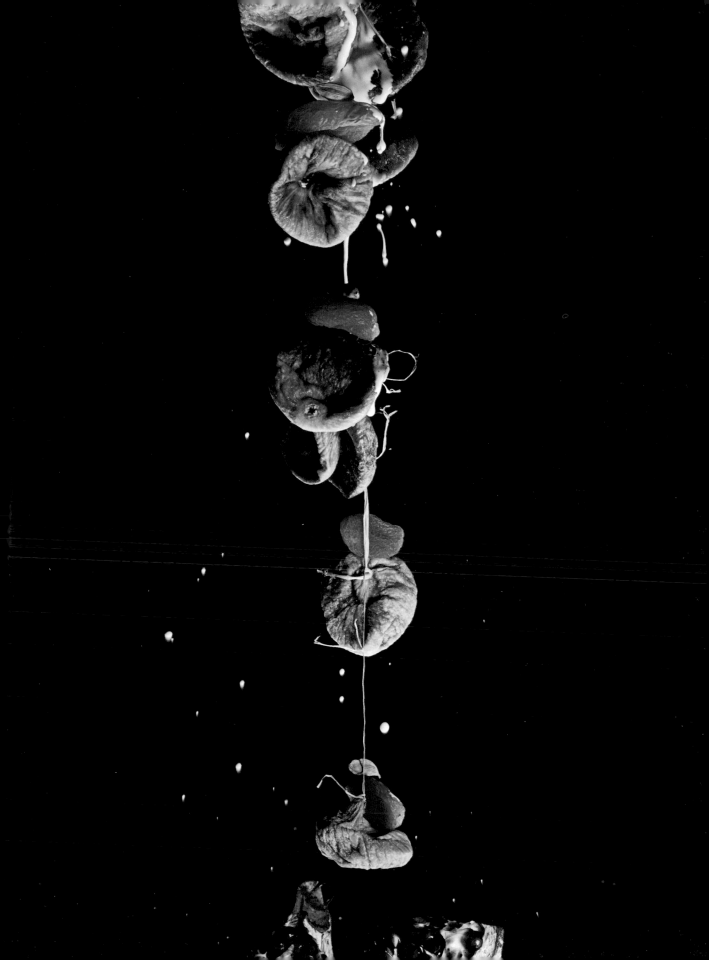

NOT ALL JAMS NEED TO BE SWEET. This tangy blend works as a topping for cheese-smeared crisps, raw pizzas, or unsweetened yoghurt for an unconventional but delicious breakfast. In addition to the pine nuts, I sometimes add chopped fresh mint, parsley, basil, or oregano as a garnish.

SUMAC TOMATO JAM WITH PINE NUTS

MAKES 2 CUPS

1½ cups warm water

1 cup unsalted sun-dried tomatoes

1 garlic clove

1 tablespoon ground sumac

¼ teaspoon ground cumin

½ teaspoon apple cider vinegar

¼ teaspoon pink salt

¼ cup extra-virgin olive oil

2 tablespoons pine nuts, for garnish

Pour the warm water over the sun-dried tomatoes and soak overnight. The next day, drain the tomatoes, reserving the soaking water. Place the tomatoes in the food processor with the garlic, sumac, cumin, vinegar, and salt and process until finely chopped. Add the oil and half the reserved soaking water. Blend until the jam is fully pureed. Transfer to a covered container and store in the refrigerator for up to 1 week. Serve garnished with the pine nuts.

I'VE TURNED MY PENCHANT FOR SNACKING and my sweet tooth into an inspiration to include more enzymes in my diet through raw treats. One of my first projects as soon as the Moon Juice kitchen was up and rolling was to create this Fig Newton–type bar.

The flavors evoke a summer evening in Bolinas, where I was cooking dinner for a group of friends that included chef Alice Waters. I went to a farm on my bicycle to buy all the produce for the meal and picked up a big basket of fresh strawberries so ripe and fragrant that I could smell them as I cycled home. That night, I macerated the berries with honey, muddled rose geraniums leaves, and scented the whipped cream with the juices.

Every time I have this bar, I remember that magical night.

STRAWBERRY ROSE GERANIUM BARS

MAKES 4

MINERALIZES DEEPLY

STRESS RELIEVER

½ recipe Vanilla Pastry Dough (page 206), chilled
1 cup Strawberry Rose Geranium Jam (page 220)

Halve the dough, then roll out one portion ¼ inch thick and spread with the jam. Roll out the remaining dough and set it on top of the jam to create a large sandwich. Dehydrate at 118°F or the closest setting on your dehydrator for 2 hours, then cool in the refrigerator. Cut into rectangles or squares. Wrap the bars tightly and store at room temperature for up to 1 week or in the freezer for up to 3 months.

THIS BROWNIE RECIPE is a good one to play with when you are making your weekly batch of Well Milk, as it is made with undehydrated pulp straight from the nut bag after straining.

Mix it up! You could add peppermint. Dried cherries. Cinnamon and chile. A tablespoon of rose water and ⅛ teaspoon cardamom, garnished with rose petals. Ginger and citrus, or any other combinations that sound delectable to you.

You could also turn this into a big cake, frost it with probiotic icing, and garnish with flowers and berries. Roll it into balls and coat them with coconut shreds, chia seeds, hemp seeds, rose petals, turmeric, and any other nuts or fruits you like.

PULP BROWNIES WITH SALTED CARAMEL SAUCE

MAKES ABOUT 5 BIG BROWNIES

10 Medjool dates, pitted
1 cup any kind of moist nut or seed pulp
¼ cup Thai coconut meat pureed in a blender until smooth
½ cup plus 1 tablespoon cacao powder, plus more for dusting
2 tablespoons almond butter, made from activated almonds
2 pinches of pink salt
1 tablespoon coconut oil
1 tablespoon nut milk (any variety)
Whipped cream (optional)
1 cup Salted Caramel Sauce (page 219)

In a food processor, combine the dates, nut or seed pulp, coconut meat, cacao, almond butter, salt, coconut oil, and nut milk and process until smooth.

Press the dough onto a dehydrator sheet in a thick layer and "bake" at 118°F or the closest setting on your dehydrator to the desired firmness, about 2 hours for a gooey, half-baked brownie or about 12 hours for a fully "baked" brownie. Dust with cacao on both sides, then cut it into squares.

To serve, place a brownie on each serving plate and top with a dollop of the cream, if using. Pour the warmed caramel sauce over all and serve immediately.

THIS RECIPE WAS CREATED FOR MY SON, Rohan—and, to be honest, for me, too. If you're not completely distracted by the fun colored sprinkles and donut shape, you can tap into the dough's subtle and sophisticated Eastern notes of sesame seeds, figs, and medicinal doses of protective chaga that create this fun and kitschy snack.

CHOCOLATE CHAGA DONUTS

MAKES 12 DONUTS

Quinoa Sprinkles
⅓ cup beet juice
⅓ cup turmeric juice
1 teaspoon coconut nectar
½ cup activated quinoa

Chaga Icing
1 tablespoon Thai coconut meat
1 teaspoon coconut nectar
½ teaspoon coconut sugar
¼ teaspoon cacao butter
½ teaspoon chaga powder
¼ teaspoon pink salt
1 teaspoon water
1½ teaspoons cacao powder

1 recipe Chia Sesame Dough
   (page 209)

Make the sprinkles: Place the beet juice and turmeric juice in 2 small bowls. Then add ½ teaspoon of coconut nectar to each bowl. Stir ¼ cup of quinoa into each bowl and set aside for 30 minutes or until the quinoa has absorbed the color from the soaking liquid. Drain the quinoa and spread on separate dehydrator sheets. Dehydrate at 118°F or the closest setting on your dehydrator for 24 hours or until dry and crunchy. The sprinkles can be stored in an airtight container for up to 3 months.

Make the icing: In a blender, combine the coconut, coconut nectar, coconut sugar, cacao butter, chaga, and salt and blend on high until creamy, scraping down the sides of the blender with a rubber spatula as needed. With the blender running on medium speed, add half the water and half the cacao powder and blend until smooth. Add the remaining water and cacao powder and blend again until smooth.

To make the donuts, soften the dough with your hands and roll it into a ½-inch-thick "snake" about 24 inches long. Pinch off a 2-inch piece and wrap the ends together to form a ring. Repeat to make 12 donuts. Place the donuts on a dehydrator sheet and dehydrate at 118°F or the closest setting on your dehydrator for 4 hours.

Spread each donut with some of the chaga icing and garnish with the sprinkles.

THESE TARTLETS WERE CREATED to combine the tantalizing flavor combination that appeared right in front of my face during a meditation: I could see them, smell them, and I knew just what they were going to taste like. I immediately went to the kitchen, summoning apricot kernel, dark cherry, and black pepper.

These blood-cleansing, plant protein–rich confections blend the flavors of sweet, sour, and spicy while reducing oxidative stress. They improve premature aging, promote optimal melatonin release, aid digestion, and support healthy circadian rhythms.

CHERRY BLACK PEPPER CUPS

MAKES 36 COOKIES

1 batch Almond Pastry Dough (page 208)
1 cup Cherry Black Pepper Jam (page 223)
Cracked black peppercorns

Roll small portions (about .5 ounce) of the dough into balls with your hands, then use your thumb to make an indentation in the center of each. With your fingers, smooth the edges of the dough and seal any large cracks. The thumbprints should be uniform in size and shape. Place the cookies on dehydrator sheets and dehydrate at 118°F or the closest setting on your dehydrator for 12 hours.

Remove the cookies from the dehydrator and fill each thumbprint with 1 teaspoon of the jam. Sprinkle 3 cracked peppercorns in the center of each filled thumbprint.

Return the cookies to the dehydrator and dehydrate for 24 hours, or until the jam is somewhat dry and glossy.

Let cool for 30 minutes. The cookies are now ready to eat or store in the refrigerator in an airtight container for up to 1 month. If you want to make them pantry-stable or ship them, return them to the dehydrator for 12 hours more, then transfer to an airtight container.

WITH THEIR CHEESY, VEGETAL NOTES, these small tarts are a perfect brunch dish. Serve them with a green leaf salad. Garnish with a nasturtium flower for an extra touch of peppery bite. I sometimes add a bit of fermented veggies as well, for even more tang and goodness.

SAVORY TART WITH CHEESE AND TOMATO JAM FILLING

SERVES 4

1 recipe Herb & Cheese Dough (page 212)

½ cup Soft Shallot & Herb Cheese (page 159)

½ cup Sumac Tomato Jam with Pine Nuts (page 227)

2 tablespoons pine nuts

2 tablespoons shredded fresh basil leaves

Handful of baby arugula

Mold the dough into small individual tartlets about 3½ inches in diameter. Dehydrate at 118°F or the closest setting on your dehydrator for 12 hours. Let cool, then fill each tartlet ½ inch full with the cheese, and top evenly with the tomato jam. Sprinkle each tartlet with pine nuts, then garnish with the basil and arugula.

CHAPTER 10

RAW CHOCOLATE

Raw chocolate, made from ground raw cacao beans, is the starship to launch a thousand recipes, allowing you to make sweets and confections that not only appease your sweet tooth, but deliver beneficial antioxidants, mood-boosting hormones, and a lovely dose of endorphins that increase brain flow, battle fatigue, and spark libido.

I make raw chocolate in large batches and break it into chunks, storing most of it in a tightly sealed container in the refrigerator. The rest I place in a glass jar that I keep on my stovetop next to my salt and pepper. This jar has become a mythic element in my kitchen, a bottomless jar of chocolate goodness that moves through many stages in a day. When the weather is cold it becomes a jar of hardened chocolate; in summer months it will remain softer. When I turn the oven on and leave the jar on top of my range, the chocolate liquefies. In the spring and fall it has a fudgy consistency that begs me to eat a spoonful straight out of the jar every time I pass by. Each time the jar becomes depleted, I replenish it with a few more chunks from the fridge.

The two tools I love for working with chocolate are a tongue depressor and toothpicks. The tongue depressor allows me to drop a ball of icing, dough, or cheese into my chocolate, roll it around, and transfer it to a plate to set, or spread chocolate in a tart shell. Toothpicks are perfect for dipping dried fruits and other small items into molten chocolate.

For an impressive dessert you can make a tart shell (page 206), add a layer of Soft Cheese Base (sweetened or not, as you like), and top it with a glaze of chocolate. You could do the same thing with any of the jams, making one large tart or miniature thumbprint tartlets.

THIS MASTER RECIPE is a mainstay in my kitchen and can be used to dip cookies or dried fruits; to make candies, barks, and bonbons; or as a filling for cookies or tarts. It's a perfect palette for embellishing with adaptogenic herbs.

JOY
PROMOTER

BRAIN
ACTIVATOR

MASTER CHOCOLATE RECIPE FOR DIPPING, POURING, CANDY MAKING & SNACKING

MAKES ABOUT 2 CUPS

1½ cups cacao paste
¾ cup cacao butter
1½ teaspoons raw vanilla bean
    powder
2 teaspoons coconut nectar

In a double boiler, melt the cacao paste, cacao butter, and vanilla over barely simmering water, stirring until smooth. Pour the melted mixture into a blender, add the coconut nectar, and blend until smooth. Transfer to a shallow container to cool, then refrigerate until firm. Break into chunks and store at room temperature for up to 5 days or in the refrigerator in an airtight container for up to 1 month.

THINGS TO DIP IN CHOCOLATE

Bring this chocolate up to dipping consistency by setting the jar in a pot of warm water until it becomes fluid. Then rummage around the kitchen and see what you can dip in it. Those frozen avocados that you have in the freezer for shakes are absolutely divine dipped in chocolate, as is any dried fruit you may have, especially dried bananas and mango. Obviously any cookies you've made with one of our pastry doughs are 1,000 times better dipped in chocolate; undehydrated balls of dough dipped in chocolate make for a chocolate-covered donut hole cookie dough experience. One of my favorite treats is dipping the nasturtium flowers and leaves that grow in my yard into chocolate; it's a dark chocolate, peppery, floral delicacy that looks beautiful and tastes amazing. (I would recommend treating any edible flower this way.) Another trick is taking some of the Soft Cheese Base you may have in the fridge and hand-rolling it into balls to dip. Dip a few big chunks of the Salted Maple Reishi Granola (page 177) in chocolate or stuff a medjool date with a bit of the Carrot Gingerbread Dough (page 211) and dunk the whole thing. All of these need to go in the refrigerator for a few minutes to harden, and then can be transferred to a container and stored in the fridge.

FROZEN AVOCADO WEDGES

FROZEN BANANAS

WHOLE FRESH FRUIT CHUNKS

EDIBLE FLOWERS

ANY OF THE SWEET DOUGHS HAND-ROLLED INTO TRUFFLE-SIZED BALLS

COOKIES, DEHYDRATED UNTIL CRISP

MEDJOOL DATES PITTED AND FILLED WITH ICING OR NUT BUTTER

MOON BARKS

If you pour 2 cups of liquefied chocolate onto a plate or baking sheet and allow it to harden, you will have created a bark. I like to spike my barks with an adaptogen, then sprinkle the surface with one or two garnishes. In five minutes you can bulk up for a full quarter of the year's chocolate eating and gifting in one fell swoop. It's fun to make in front of or with guests who will not only be buzzed from the chocolate blend but also be thoroughly impressed with your live chocolate show.

Reheat the chocolate in a double boiler, stirring frequently, until just fluid enough to pour. Stir in one or two potent powders of your choosing.

Pour the chocolate onto a dinner plate. Sprinkle with your preferred garnishes, and freeze for about 20 minutes, or until firm. When ready, pop the bark off the dish with a butter knife and break it into pieces.

POTENT POWDERS:
ashwaganda; chaga; cordyceps, ho shou wu; maca; pearl; reishi; shisandra; lucuma; matcha; mucuna; raw vanilla powder, cardamom; cinnamon; mesquite

GARNISHES:
cacao nibs; hemp or chia seeds; nuts or seeds; shredded coconut; flower petals; chopped dried fruit; bee pollen; granola; quinoa sprinkles

MATCHA ROSE BEAUTY BARK
Add 1 teaspoon matcha, ½ teaspoon pearl powder; garnish with 2 tablespoons dried rose petals.

DEEP CHOCOLATE RADIANCE BARK
Add ½ teaspoon ground cinnamon, 2 teaspoons ho shou wu, garnish with cacao nibs.

BLACK FOREST IMMUNITY BARK
Add 2 teaspoons chaga, 1 teaspoon reishi; garnish with ½ cup dried sour cherries.

FIGGY POWER BARK
Add 2 teaspoons cordyceps, 1 tablespoon maca; garnish with ½ cup chopped Turkish figs.

KUMQUAT TRANQUILITY BARK
Add 2 teaspoons ashwaganda, ¼ teaspoon ground cardamom; garnish with 4 kumquats, thinly sliced.

STRAWBERRY SEX BARK
1 teaspoon schizandra, 1 teaspoon ho shou wu; garnish with ½ cup chopped freeze-dried strawberries.

BON BONS

If you want to encase something soft in chocolate, you can make bon-bons using small candy molds readily available at cookware stores and some craft shops. These can be any size but I prefer those with about a 1-ounce capacity. Put any decorative elements, such as bee pollen, bright green pistachios, or a rose petal, that you want to show on the finished bonbon into the mold first. Then add a small dab of cheese, jam, nut butter, frosting, or herbs and fill the mold to the top with molten dipping chocolate. Place them in the refrigerator until set (or in the freezer to expedite the process). Unmold your bonbons and store them in a covered container in the refrigerator.

If you want your bonbons to have a smooth chocolate top and encase your filling completely, fill the molds about one-third full with chocolate and let the chocolate firm up in the fridge for 15 or 20 minutes. When it's hardened, carefully spoon your filling onto the center of each bonbon (don't cover the whole surface or the filling will show on the sides) leaving at least a quarter of the depth empty. Fill the mold with chocolate, completely encapsulating the filling, and chill again until hardened. Unmold and store as above. Once you've tried this easy process a few times, you'll want to play with different flavorings and combinations. The possibilities are literally unlimited, but here are a few suggested pairings to get you started.

CHERRY JAM AND BLACK PEPPER ASHWAGANDA

MATCHA AND SESAME BUTTER

DRIED APRICOT AND PISTACHIOS

CHEESE AND BEE POLLEN

HONEY, SEA SALT, COCONUT OIL WHIPPED TOGETHER

MACA, CARDAMOM, ALMOND BUTTER

ROSE WATER, COCONUT BUTTER, ROSE PETALS, PISTACHIO

BUTTER-CREAM ICING, STRAWBERRY ROSE GERANIUM JAM

PINE NUTS AND FIG JAM

BANANA PUREE, MACA MESQUITE WALNUTS, AND MUCUNA

ACKNOWLEDGMENTS

Thanks go to the following, whose help was invaluable in creating this book:

    Moon Juice's kitchen crew: Leo, Blanca, and Giselle;

    My savvy and supportive agent, Nicole;

    My ever-patient, genius editor, Pam;

    My clairvoyant photographer, John;

    My talented graphic designers, Marysarah and Heather;

    The left-brain queens, Lilly and Kim;

    And thank you to the patrons and employees who have been a part of building Moon Juice from the very first day, as well as those yet to come. Moon Juice has been a mission that I cognized and was first on the job but it is certainly a force of its own that's nourished and sustained by everyone who has ever joined the ranks and participated daily in the cosmic indulgence.

    And lastly, to Rohan, who has uniquely inspired me to keep going and to always get better.

INDEX